THE LIFE OF
MOSES

THE LIFE OF
MOSES

EDMOND FLEG

Translated from the French
by Stephen Haden Guest

Hope Publishing House
Pasadena, California

This book is a revised and updated edition of the original title translated from M. Fleg's manuscript *La Vie de Moïse,* published by *La Nouvelle Revue Fran-çaise,* Paris, 1928.

Copyright © 1995, Hope Publishing House

Hope Publishing House
P.O. Box 60008
Pasadena, CA 91116
Tel: (818) 792-6123 / Fax: (818) 792-2121

ISBN 0-932727-82-4, trade paperback, $12.95
ISBN 0-932727-84-0, library hardcover, $19.95

Front Cover: *Moses and the Burning Bush,* 13th Century Icon
at the Mount St. Catherine's Monastery,
Mt. Sinai, Egypt

**Library of Congress
Cataloging-in-Publication Data**

Fleg, Edmond, 1874-1963
    [Vie de Moise. English]
    The life of Moses / Edmond Fleg ; translated from the French by Stephen Haden Guest. -- Rev. and updated ed.
        p.   cm.
    Summary: A compilation of Midrash, Biblical, and legendary stories about the prophet Moses, who led the Children of Israel out of slavery in Egypt.
    ISBN 0-932727-82-4 (trade paper : alk. paper). -- ISBN 0-932727-84-0 (library hardcover : alk. paper)
    1. Moses (Biblical leader)--Juvenile literature. 2. Bible. O.T.--Biography--Juvenile literature. [1. Moses (Biblical leader)]
    I. Title.
BS580.M6F62 1995
222'.1092--dc20   95-22612
[B]   CIP
                                                                                            AC

Translator's Note

Edmond Fleg is a poet, so that to translate any of his works would be hard enough, but this work—the vision of Moses, the servant of God, as it has come down through 4,000 years of Jewish tradition—presents two peculiar difficulties. First, the problem M. Fleg has himself solved so exquisitely, but which has to be solved anew in a translation, is to combine into a harmonious style the loftiest passages of the Bible with the vivid, half-magical imaginations of some of the early Palestinian and Babylonian rabbis plus the profound, enigmatic mysticism of some and the shrewd, practical, juristic or everyday commentary of others. Second, a problem arising for the translator *into English*—is the language of the Authorized Version.

The first problem[1] confronts every writer who deals with the magnificent language of the Hebrew Bible wherein much is left to be worked out by the imagination of the hearer, in conjunction with the fuller, more elaborate style of the rabbis. The second problem is that in certain parts of the book the translator suffers from direct comparison with the inspired Authorized Version, for sometimes the first half of a sentence is taken from the Bible word for word and the second half is an addition, with or without transmutation, from the Midrash, or an original extension of the Biblical idea by M. Fleg himself, and sometimes one of the best-known Biblical passages is taken and so paraphrased or expanded by the inclusion of material from the Tradition, that the Bible narrative cannot be used in a conscientious rendering, though its

---

[1] This question is admirably discussed in the Introduction to *The Parables and Similes of the Rabbis: Agricultural and Pastoral,* by Rabbi Asher Feldman. A most interesting work.

majestic reverberation in the reader's memory must inevitably make the paraphrase seem somewhat flat.

A great—and in part insuperable—difficulty exists only for the translator into English, for the French Bible, though it has unique beauties of its own—*Comme un cerf brame après des eaux courantes, ainsi mon âme soupire après toi ô Dieu!*—is as a whole nothing more than a reverent, dignified rendering of an obviously foreign idiom. With the possible exception of the Lutheran Bible, the Authorized Version alone in the world has influenced the whole literature, the whole imagination of a people for 300 years—so that the Star of Jacob and the burning bush and the law for the widow and the orphan have become part of the poetic fibre of the English language. When, therefore, that part of Balaam's prophecy immediately preceding the Star of Jacob is given in unfamiliar form, the reader cannot help feeling a certain loss and confusion. Yet perhaps there is some compensation even here, for new elements are added to the familiar narrative and the very strangeness may, as with the retranslations of the Bible into modern idiom, serve to make the Authorized Version fresher and clearer.

Thus the translator was uncertain about the best idiom to adopt—for the language of the Authorized Version could not be intermingled in the same paragraph with a simple, though poetic, modern prose, as could the French Bible with the modern French. Modern versions of the Bible such as Dr. Moffatt's, sincere and illuminating as they are, offer less help than might be thought.

The translators of the Authorized Version, to whom the Bible in the common tongue was still a strange thing—whereas to the Jews it had been daily bread through the centuries—sometimes refused to see that certain passages in the all-inclusive Book were prosaic and meant to be prosaic. The early translators were determined to lift every part to the utmost intensity and thus sometimes mistranslated, but present-day translators who call Princes

Sheikhs, Elders *Notables* and miters *turbans,* with syntax to match, really misrepresent far more seriously, however great their scholarship and piety—for the Bible is God's Word to his people and the total effect in English as in Hebrew should be dignified but clear.

The translator has, however, followed Dr. Moffatt[2] to a certain extent, for example by using *Eternal* in a good many places where the Authorized Version has *Lord* (which should, really, be used relatively infrequently) and when *Pharaoh* or the *Egyptians* are speaking by using *Hebrews* instead of *Israelites.*

For the rabbinic names he has adopted the modern spelling, using *h* for *ch*—this *h* should be pronounced something like the final *ch* in the Scots *loch.* Various technical matters have been referred to Mr. Paul Goodman and to Mr. Jacob Hodess, scholars to whom the translator's sincere thanks are due, but he alone is responsible for the choices made.

This tedious list of the difficulties that had to be overcome is not meant to excuse the translator, but to do justice to M. Fleg's achievement. In a style apparently very simple, almost at times naïve, yet most subtly woven of clear, almost Greek perception and deep, imaginative sympathy, he does make Moses, the man of God, at whose death the earth and the heaven and the Lord God himself wept, saying, *There shall be no other Moses,* emerge from the ages a figure no less impressive than in the Bible story. But his most sensitive modern mind, penetrating the ever-living tradition of 4,000 years, reveals, through all the legends, the "simple man, humble in his heart," wistful in his human affections.

—S.H.G.

[The spellings, obsolete words and some syntax of this 1928 translation have been updated to make for ease of reading to the modern person.
—F.A.S., Pasadena, California, 1995]

[2] *A New Translation of the Bible,* by James Moffatt, D.D., D.LITT., M.A.

Author's Preface

I have the utmost respect for the learned. If, leaving aside the question of a divine revelation, their methods could reconstruct for us a true life of Moses, I would read it gladly. But, in the present state of *science*, all they could offer us as a life of Moses would scarcely be more than a mass of hazardous assertion and unverifiable conjecture.

Must we, then, here simply repeat the Bible narrative, robbing it of its beauty? By no means. In the creative memory of Israel the Biblical Moses lives on, transfigured by a tradition rich in wonderful legends. While *critical* exegesis, tracing back myths and rites to their supposed origins, would lead us to a primitive, savage Moses, wholly alien to our world of today, the religious, moral, poetical and satirical exegesis of our rabbis has, with its symbols and its anachronisms, drawn the prophet nearer to us from century to century.

Doubtless the real life of Moses will never be known *scientifically*—but is not this life, as Israel has imagined it, interpreted it and felt it through the ages, also history? And is this history ended? Has not Israel the right still to prolong it?

The very humble heir of the storytellers of the Talmud, of their spirit and their language, gathering their scattered fables, regrouping, rethinking and recasting them and, where need was, paraphrasing in my turn their paraphrases, I have tried to follow in their footsteps and continue after their fashion the tradition they have perpetuated, so that I might write this story as it now relives in me.

In this attempt to make the past live on into the present I do not think I have in any way betrayed the spirit of the texts, but neither have I tried to follow them word for word. In the manner of our rabbis, I have imagined and created, or sometimes added variants to the occasionally numerous versions they give us of a single episode. The experts may take offense. But at least let them know that I have acted from choice, not ignorance, and that my liberties with the Talmud in no way surpass the Talmud's own with the Bible.

—Edmond Fleg

Contents

The life of Moses, the man of God, is in the Holy Scriptures. But, as our Talmud teaches, the word of the Lord has more than one meaning—beneath the sacred words they read and re-read, our sages discovered many secrets not for the eyes of fools and, beneath the known facts, many unknown, out of which they made the tales which made this tale.

CHAPTER I

PHARAOH'S DREAM

It is written: *There rose up a new king over Egypt, which did not know Joseph and he said unto his people, "Behold, the people of the children of Israel are more and mightier than we...."*

And concerning this our teachers tell us that in the 353rd year after the coming of the children of Israel into the land of Egypt, Pharaoh dreamed a dream.

In this dream he was seated upon his throne and he lifted up his eyes. Two fingers came out of the darkness. Between these fingers there shined a rod, longer than a sunbeam. Hung from this rod were two pans of weighing-scales—one, which was below, was of gold and vast as a continent; the other, which was high up, was of plaited straw and little as a bird's nest.

He saw upon the pan of gold the likeness of a river and going up from this river, harvests and harvesters, warriors and chariots, cities and pyramids, and going up from these pyramids, kings and queens.

Then he saw upon the pan of straw a newborn child.

As the pan of gold with the river and the harvests, the warriors and the cities, the pyramids and the kings, rose, the pan of straw came lower, came lower as if the child were heavier than all the land of Egypt, all its harvesters, all its warriors and all its rulers.

In the anguish of his heart Pharaoh awoke—it was a dream. He called his counselors and told them his dream.

Now, according to Rabbi Simon, these counselors were three prophets—Balaam, son of Beor, from the land of the Two Rivers;

Job, the man of Uz; and Jethro, the Midianite. For, our doctors say, the nations, just like Israel, have prophets to whom the Holy One, blessèd be he, shows the truth; but they cannot see in it, as can the prophets of Israel, the heart of the Eternal.

Balaam, son of Beor, spoke first and said, "A mother comes and goes about her business, who bears within her womb the liberator of Israel. Take care, O King. He will destroy this land with all who dwell in it, if you do not first destroy Israel."

"Destroy Israel?" Pharaoh answered him, "We have long talked about it. When you came to me, with the master of my chariots, to say, 'Rise up against the children of this people, who dwell in your midst, before they become too numerous and make alliance with your enemies,' I replied, you remember, 'You are fools. Our ancestors were saved from famine by Joseph, their ancestor; without these Hebrews we would not be eating now; and you would have me rise up against them?' What did my warriors then? They seized away my throne and my crown, until I had said, 'Be it so. I will rise up against these Hebrews.'

"I took their corn and their fields—still they increased and multiplied. I bowed them beneath the whip of the slave-master, I made them bake bricks in the sun, roll down the stone for the pyramid, dig canals for the abundance of my waters and raise walls around my cities—still they increased and multiplied. I ordered their midwives to strangle their children as they were delivered from the womb—still they increased and multiplied. They were 70 when they came with Jacob into the land of Egypt; now their number is 600,000. And you tell me, 'Destroy the children of Israel.' Rather, tell me how."

Balaam, son of Beor, answered, "By fire we can in no wise destroy them, for their God saved their ancestor Abraham from the fire and by fire he would punish us. By the sword we can in no wise destroy them, for their God saved their father Isaac from the sword and by the sword he would punish us. By bondage we can in no wise destroy them, for their God saved from bondage their father Jacob and by bondage he would punish us. We shall destroy them by water. Their God, in truth, saved Noah from the Flood, but he will not punish us by water for he swore after the Flood that the waters should no more cover the earth. Therefore, command that every son that is newborn to the Hebrew women be cast into the river."

Having heard these words, Pharaoh turned to Job the man of Uz and asked him, "What do you think of this?" But Job looked up and looked down and refused to say a word. Then Pharaoh questioned Jethro the Midianite, who in his turn spoke, saying:

"Their God has sworn not to unloose the Flood upon the whole earth again, but has he sworn not to unloose it upon a part of the earth, upon Egypt? You were wise; be wise again, O Pharaoh. Let these Hebrews be. In bondage and humiliation they are still mighty, for mighty is their God."

"You would have my crown seized from me once more?" cried Pharaoh. "I have the bull-god, the jackal-god, the snake-god, the lion-god, the monkey-god, the crocodile-god—I have a thousand gods; I am the lord of all these gods. Am I not able to do anything against these Israelites who have but one God? From this day forth let all the newborn male children in Israel be taken and let them be thrown into the river."

When he had spoken, the evil Balaam rejoiced in his heart; Job was silent; but Jethro the Midianite, fearing the anger of Pharaoh, fled from before his face into the land of Midian.

And, comments Rabbi Simon, because Job had not spoken, he was visited by great torments; because Balaam had spoken for Israel's death, he died a bloody death; and because Jethro had spoken for Israel's life, his sons' sons sat in the Sanhedrin.

CHAPTER II

THE CHILD SAVED FROM THE WATER

After the death of Joseph and his brothers, the Hebrews in the land of Egypt, grazing their flocks in the pastures of Goshen, ceased to walk in the ways of the Lord. No longer carving in their children's flesh the sign of the covenant made by their ancestors with the Holy One, blessèd be he, they said, "Let us be like the Egyptians," and, like the Egyptians, they worshipped gods with animal faces. It was for this that the Lord had changed the love of the Egyptians into hate and permitted them to make slaves of those who were no longer his servants.

One tribe alone, that of Levi, kept in their hearts the memories and hopes of Israel and, among this tribe, there was a man righteous among the righteous—Amram, husband of Jochebed, father of Aaron and of Miriam. And upon the righteousness of Amram the whole world rested.

For, our Elders have taught us, God desires his presence to dwell here below. Here it dwelt on the first day of the first man. But when Adam sinned, it went up from the first into the second heaven; and, fleeing one after the other from the generation of Enoch, of the Flood, of Babel and of Sodom, it hid itself in the third, then in the fourth, then in the fifth, then in the sixth heaven. When Sarah was defiled by Pharaoh, the presence of God took refuge in the seventh heaven. But with Abraham, Isaac and Jacob, with Levi and Kohath, it descended once more into the second heaven; now, by Amram's virtue, it sojourned on the border of the first heaven. Lo! soon, with Moses, the presence of

God was again to inhabit the earth.

Meanwhile Pharaoh's edict was carried out. The mothers of Israel, leaning over the waters, wept for their sons and the river flowed and received their tears.

Then said Amram, "Since the Israelites beget for murder, let them cease to beget." And he divorced Jochebed. And, doing as he had done, all the men in Israel repudiated their wives.

But the spirit of wisdom and vision was already upon Miriam. She dared to speak before Amram her father, saying, "Crueler than Pharaoh's is your decree. The Egyptian condemns only the male children, but you strike the daughters with the sons. He deprives his victims of earthly life only; you, who prevent them from being born, deprive them also of the resurrection."

These words enlightened Amram; doubtless he knew our proverb: *Your child can give you more than one lesson.* He told the Israelites to take back their wives and he himself, taking back Jochebed, led her for the second time beneath the nuptial canopy. Miriam and Aaron danced at their new marriage-keeping. Thus was Moses conceived.

Now from month to month Jochebed regained her youth—the lines vanished from her face, her limbs exhaled the fragrance of flowers and her womb bore in joy the promise of its fruit.

But Amram was sad in his heart. Before each Hebrew's house where a mother awaited the coming of a child, Pharaoh posted two armed guards. Whoever hid away a newborn male child from the watery death, he and all his house perished by the bloody death. So Amram thought, "If there is born to me a son, what will become of my son?"

In the sleep of the night he, in his turn, had a dream. In this dream he was standing on the shore of the river; his lowered eyes were looking at the waves, which, becoming transparent, flowed like a river of air. At the bottom there lay, in thousands and in myriads, one against the other, the corpses of sucklings. Suddenly, behold, living, upon the bank, a child walking—his two small hands stretched out toward the water. Then something quivered among the corpses in the depths—a motion passed through them, swayed them, raised them to their feet; they quickened; they grew; they came forth out of the waves; they were a people who rose up and who sang, "He is born who will deliver us; his name shall live in eternity."

At the voices crying out Amram awoke. A light filled the room. Jochebed, three months before the expected day, had given birth, but without pain, for, say our sages, the curse which Eve had caused aforetime weighs not upon the virtuous mother. Miriam smiled, presenting the child, born circumcised, to his father and she prophesied, saying, "Behold the salvation of Israel!"

Three times the moon waxed and waned and they had not revealed to the Egyptians the miraculous son. Now the day approached when his birth would be discovered. They resolved to entrust him to the waters of the river and to the protection of God. Jochebed made an ark of bulrushes and daubed it with pitch without and clay within. She put the child in that rough cradle, having entreated the help of the Most High and laid it, with trembling hands, among the flags by the river's brink. And while she, weeping, returned to Amram, Miriam upon the bank followed the ark with her eyes as the waves took it and watched what would come of her prophecy.

What wonders does Providence have in store for Israel! Who could have thought that Abraham would have begotten in his old age?—that Jacob, having but a rod when he passed over Jordan, would return laden with riches and with blessings? Who could have believed that Joseph, chained in the prisons of Egypt, would one day reign over the Egyptians? Who could have hoped that a child, lost upon the swell of a vast river, would save a people and all humankind? Yet that was Miriam's hope.

According to Rabbi Hanina bar Papa, that was the 21st day of the month of Nisan and the ministering angels said before the Lord, "King of the World, will you permit that on this day of Nisan, whereon your Song of the Divided Waters is to be sung, there shall perish the one who is to sing it?"

According to Rabbi Aha bar Hanina, that day was the sixth of the month of Sivan and the ministering angels said before the Lord, "King of the World, will you permit that on this day of Sivan, whereon you are to give your law on Sinai, there shall perish the one who is to receive it?"

While the angels were talking, Bithiah, the daughter of Pharaoh, came down to the river with her maidens. She was white with leprosy from head to foot, and her leprosy made her barren. Each day she bathed in the waters of the river, wishing to leave in them her leprosy and her barrenness which deprived Pharaoh of posterity and his crown of succession.

When she saw the slight thing floating upon the waves, Bithiah sent a maid to fetch it. The maid swam toward the thing and as she was slow to reach it, her arms, miraculously, were lengthened. When Pharaoh's daughter opened the ark, behold, in the ark was a light, the presence of God. Beneath the light there was a circumcised babe, a Hebrew.

The maid said, "Mistress, will you save a Hebrew? When a king commands, his daughter obeys."

But Bithiah was already touching the child with her hand and, suddenly, the whiteness of leprosy fell from her flesh; the princess was pure as the newborn babe. She felt she would cherish him more than a son of her womb. And she called him Moses, *The Withdrawn*, saying, "Because I drew him out of the water."

Miriam approached. The babe needed a nurse. She suggested she should seek one out from among the mourning mothers of Israel for, say our doctors, the mouth that was one day to converse with the Lord could not defile itself with the impure milk of an Egyptian. The nurse she brought was Jochebed. Bithiah entrusted to her him whom, in her heart, she had already placed upon the throne. Then, pretending to be with child, she announced an heir to Pharaoh.

Custom decreed that he should not be presented at court until the end of his third year, so for three years Jochebed could cherish her redeemed son, rocking him to the songs of Israel, while Amram, Aaron and Miriam in joy beheld his increasing beauty.

When the time came, Bithiah, holding the child in her arms, went up the avenue of sphinxes that lead to the royal pylon. It was the day whereon the vanquished of the north and of the south brought to Pharaoh their tribute of ebony and palms, of turquoise and of incense, of ivory and of gold. On their knees before him, slaves, princes, priests, sorcerers snuffed up the dust. Among them were Balaam and Job, the seers of the nations, who, abandoned by Jethro, now alone enlightened the king with their blind wisdom.

Smiling at the smile of his seed, Pharaoh wished to caress the child. But the boy, his small hands filled by an extraordinary strength, took the crown from the royal head and set it upon his own. "Here," said Pharaoh, "is a young prince exceedingly eager to reign!"

"He must," Balaam cried, "be thrown into the water!"

"Again?" Pharaoh answered him. "Didn't you read in the stars, more than three years ago, that the threatening child of my dream was at last in the river? Since that day I have not drowned the children. And you want me to begin the drowning again?"

"Strangle him, if you prefer that," answered Balaam, "but save your head from this ravisher of crowns."

"But does he know what he is doing, at his age?" murmured Bithiah.

"And what do you think of it, Job?" Pharaoh demanded.

Job looked up and looked down and answered, "If he knows what he does, let him die. Let him live, if he knows not."

"But how can we know if he knows or knows not?"

Job looked up and looked down and answered no word.

"Let two dishes be presented to him," said Balaam. "On one let there be scattered burning coals; on the other pieces of gold. If he takes the coal, your crown is safe—he knows not what he does. But if he takes the gold, fear him; he has understanding."

Balaam thought that a child already so clever would not burn his fingers. In fact, the child did want to touch the gold, but the angel Gabriel, who was watching over, turned aside his hand. Moses grasped a lighted coal and carried it to his mouth. Thus, say our rabbis, for this reason he was slow of speech and of a slow tongue all the days of his life.

Bithiah uttered a cry. Pharaoh laughed a great laugh. Job, the prudent, returned to Uz, the city of his birth. Balaam returned, vexed, to the land of the Two Rivers.

It was thus that Moses, through whom Egypt was to perish, became a prince over all the princes of the Egyptians.

CHAPTER III

THE SON OF BITHIAH

It is written: *And he became her son* ... But the childhood of this son and his youth—what were they? A rabbi, who will not give us his name, tells us the following, citing Philo the thinker and Josephus the historian as sources.

When Moses had come of age to learn, this future sovereign had for teachers the wisest readers of images.

Some taught him the names of the gods: Hathor, the fostering cow; the bull Hap, born of a virgin heifer; Anubis, the jackal that embalms the dead; the hawk Horus; the serpent Apepi; Shu, the sun; the earth, Seb; and Nut, the sky; the nine gods of Memphis, the nine gods of Thebes; all the gods of every space and place.

Moses learned the names of the gods, but at night upon his ivory couch there awakened in his heart the songs once sung by Jochebed, his foster-nurse, who sang of a God that has no head of a beast, nor face of a man, nor starry rays, nor color of sun, a God who is not seen and who is everywhere and Who Alone Is God.

Others taught him the history of the Pharaohs; of those who had imprisoned the Nile in its canals and stored up in their granaries during the plentiful years; of those who had hewn into colossi rocks of porphyry and seated statues in their temples; of those who had annihilated whole peoples and trod the whole world beneath their feet.

Moses recited the history of the Pharaohs. But at night, upon his ivory couch, the songs of Jochebed awoke in his heart and sang of a people who had no harvest nor statues nor slaves bowed beneath them, a people of slaves, suckled with anguish.

Others taught him the duties of kings, saying, "Don your panoply of war: shatter the nations; cut down figs and vines; burn the cities; massacre in myriads."

Moses repeated the duty of kings. But at night, upon his ivory couch, the songs of Jochebed awakened in his heart, singing, "Be prudent like Jacob, be gentle like Isaac, be faithful like Abraham."

Sometimes Bithiah, whom he believed to be his mother, took him to prayer. Embellished in red, she presented an offering to the idol embellished in blue. Moses did not pray; he pondered, "How does one pray to the God whom one cannot see?"

Sometimes the princes, whom he thought were his cousins, took him to the games. They threw the disc of ball; they advanced their pawns; they shook the dice. Moses did not play. He pondered, "Where does this dolorous people suffer?"

Sometimes Pharaoh, whom he thought was his grandfather, took him to the council of his counselors. Seated upon his throne, the sovereign listened to the elder of his priests, or the steward of his treasures. Moses did not listen. He pondered, "Of whom did Abraham the faithful, Isaac the gentle and Jacob the prudent take counsel?"

When he was old enough for war, Moses received the assignment of vanquishing the rebellious Ethiopians. For nine years the warriors of Egypt had vainly besieged their king, Kikanos, in his city of Sheba. To the east and the north this city was defended by high walls; on the west a river protected it; on the south a space was guarded by serpents.

The first Egyptian general had attacked the city by the walls, felling forests to build towers from which his archers shot their arrows. But Kikanos had shattered the towers and the archers beneath a hail of basalt. The second general, trying to take the city from the river, had built a fleet of rafts to cross the swift waters. But, drawn on by whirlpools to the cataracts, the rafts and their rowers had disappeared. A third had advanced with his chariots among the serpents. But, writhing up into the air their millions of coils, with gaping mouths, the serpents had swallowed up horses and charioteers.

When Moses had brought up his fresh troops, Tharbis, the daughter of Kikanos, beheld him one day from the top of the rampart. Now he was of great stature and had a shining countenance. Tharbis loved him and sent word to him, "Be my spouse. I give you my city and my beauty."

But Moses, in whom perpetually there sang the songs of Jochebed, remembered Sarah, who was a serving woman, and Rebecca and Rachel, who were shepherdesses; and he did not desire the daughter of a king as his wife.

His soldiers, who had followed his orders and captured countless ibises, now loosed them upon the serpents, whose eyes and hearts they pierced. Moses and the army, crossing upon their corpses, entered the citadel. All Ethiopia was beneath the soles of his feet and he returned into the land of Egypt bringing back treasures of ebony and of ivory, of plumes and of gems, of tame monkeys and of dancing dwarfs.

Then Pharaoh, calling Moses to his throne, put in his hands the double whip and upon his head the double crown. Followed by a cortège of warriors and priests, standing upon his silver chariot, Moses swept forth, acclaimed by the multitudes, through the kingdom of the south and the kingdom of the north.

One day, as he was going in his glory along the borders of the land of Goshen, he saw beside the road some men who were groaning. He was told, "These are Hebrews." He descended from his chariot; he threw away his double whip and his double crown and he went with the slaves.

Then a Voice spoke from out the void saying, "Since you leave your royalty for my people, since for them you descend into slavery, for you I will leave my heaven and I will come down upon earth."

Hard was their bondage. Throughout every day, through every night, the children of Israel toiled. Some, with straw and damped clay, molded bricks; others dug trenches which, before they were scarce dug, filled again; others built houses and cities which, before they were finished, collapsed. Plague devoured them; their thickly piled corpses, that could not be mourned nor buried, rotted upon the ground, the stench of the dead killing the living. And Moses thought, "What have they done to deserve their wretchedness?"

According to Rabbi Jehudah, ten strong things were created in the world: rock is strong, but iron cleaves it; iron is strong, but fire melts it; fire is strong, but water quenches it; water is strong, but clouds bear it away; clouds are strong, but winds drive them; winds are strong, but humans resist them; humans are strong, but fear casts them down; fear is strong, but wine casts it out; wine is strong, but sleep dissolves it; sleep is strong, but death is stronger. And loving-kindness is stronger yet, for it survives death. Now Moses was filled with loving-kindness.

He said to the Israelites, "My people, my loved ones, alas for you, alas for me! To save you from death, would that I might die!" And for them he molded bricks and bore burdens, for them he buried the dead. The songs that Jochebed had once sung awoke in his heart, singing of a Messiah of peace and justice who shall come, one day, to save humankind. And Moses pondered, "Why comes he not to save these Hebrews?"

One night as he sought to comfort their distress, other comfortings mingled with his own: Moses knew again the voice of Jochebed. With Amram, Aaron and Miriam he journeyed throughout the land of Goshen, all four reminding the children of Israel of the invisible God they had forsaken. But the Israelites would not listen; they spat upon them to show their disgust or else, drunk with sudden folly, they laughed and jumped and somersaulted. Others gathered the piled bricks and threw them at the heads of those who brought them God. And Moses pondered, "Is this why they deserve their wretchedness?"

Then he learned from his father and mother the secret of his birth, the ark of rushes that saved him from the waters, Pharaoh's decree, the centuries of bondage, the forgotten greatness of Jacob and of Joseph, the land of milk and honey trod by the Patriarchs and promised by God to their seed. He learned that a savior would arise for Israel. Miriam prophesied, "You will be this savior." But he did not believe her; for he was a simple man and humble in his heart.

CHAPTER IV

THE FLIGHT INTO MIDIAN

It is written: *Moses saw an Egyptian smiting a Hebrew ...*"
Our sages have said of this, "Consider the instinct of evil; it is
willed by God, for without willing it, it serves the will of God."

Pharaoh had placed over each ten Israelites an Israelite as
foreman. Dathan, son of Pallu, was one of them. Over each ten
Israelite foremen was an Egyptian taskmaster. Maror the Egyptian
was one of them. These taskmasters were all cruel and Maror
cruelest of all.

Now Dathan had a wife, Shelomith, daughter of Dibri, of the
tribe of Dan. Shelomith was beautiful; Maror coveted her. One
day, before dawn, he came, had Dathan put in chains and, in front
of him, took his pleasure of Shelomith's beauty. Dathan repudiated his wife. But from that day Maror was yet more cruel; he
struck Dathan, he sought his death.

Moses, having seen this injustice, raged in his soul: as Maror
raised his whip over Dathan, he slew him. How could Moses kill,
our rabbis ask? Is it not written: *You shall not kill?* But, they
answer, Moses had thought in his anger of the justice of God and
this thought was so strong that it slew the Egyptian.

When the Egyptian was dead, Moses hid him in the sand,
saying to the Israelites, "Israel is compared to the sand: as the sand
is dumb, so let your mouths be dumb."

But they were not. On the next day Dathan disputed with
Abiram, his brother. Now quarrelling comes from hatred and leads
to hatred. Moses chided them. "Young man," Dathan answered

15

him, "who has made you judge over us? Do you intend to kill us as you killed the Egyptian? Or must we go to ask Pharaoh why you are called the son of Bithiah, when you are the son of Jochebed?"

And Dathan, whose life Moses had saved, did go up to Pharaoh's palace and appeared before him, accusing Moses, "He dishonors your scepter and your crown," he said.

"Much good may it do him," answered Pharaoh.

"He strengthens your enemies, he succors your slaves."

"Much good may it do him," answered Pharaoh again.

"He is not your daughter's son; his father is a Hebrew."

At these words Pharaoh, his nostrils swollen with rage, commanded that Moses be seized and that he be put to death.

When the son of Amram heard what Dathan had done, he cried out, "O Israel, Israel, your soul is more wretched than your bondage; I know now why you have deserved such wretchedness."

Meanwhile the angels, extending their wings toward the throne on high, beseeched the Holy One, blessèd be he, "Lord, Lord, King of the World, your son is in sore distress; his doom is sealed; his scaffold is reared up; will you let him perish who is to save your people?"

The Holy One answered them, "I take him under my protection." When Pharaoh sent out his spies to arrest Moses, God made some dumb, others blind; the blind could not see where he was; the dumb, who had seen, could not speak; and Moses fled into the land of Midian.

Now Jethro, the counselor who had counseled Pharaoh to spare the Israelites, had become a priest in Midian. But having pondered in his heart and understood that the idol was vanity, he had given it back to the Midianites, saying, "I am too old; seek another priest."

In retaliation the Midianites put a ban upon him; no one would work for him; his seven daughters were his only servants, leading his flocks to pasture in the wilderness and to drink at the wells.

Every evening they arrived first and drew water for their sheep. But the evil shepherds of Midian, having come up, chased them away and watered their own beasts with the water they had drawn. One day these shepherds were yet more evil; having taken the water, they plotted to take the maidens also and, if they resisted, throw them into the well.

At that very moment Moses approached, weary from his long journey. He saw near the town the well and near the well the maidens being attacked. Alone against all he defended the maidens; then he watered Jethro's flocks as well as those of the shepherds of Midian, although they certainly in no manner deserved it. In the same way, our teachers say, Moses watered with the water of God's law, which later he gave Israel to drink—and the rest of the world also.

Consider how modest is God. Before creating humans, God consulted the angels. Moses was modest like God. When the daughters of Jethro told their father, "An Egyptian saved us," Moses did not correct them, saying, "I am a Hebrew."

Why? Did he want to hide that he was a Hebrew? In no wise, but it is like that man who had been bitten by a serpent; he ran to put his feet into water and saw that a child had fallen in. Reaching out his hand, he saved the child, who said to him, "Without you I would have lost my life."

"Not so," answered the man, "the serpent that bit me and that I fled from, going toward the water where you had fallen, is the one who saved you, not I."

In the same way, Moses thought, "It was because of the Egyptian that I was fleeing Egypt and going toward Midian where shepherds were attacking those maidens—so it is to him, not to me, that they should give thanks as their savior."

Among Jethro's daughters, Zipporah was the most modest. Looking upon her, Moses thought of Sarah, who was a serving woman, of Rebecca, of Rachel, who were shepherdesses, and he asked her to be his wife. She replied, "My father has a tree in his garden. Each man who desires one of us for wife, he commands him to pull it up and each one who tries to pull it up, the tree devours him. Will you try to pull up the tree?"

Now this tree was the rod which the Holy One, blessèd be he, had made on the eve of the first Sabbath and which Adam, the first man, received when he was expelled from Paradise. Adam transmitted it to Shem; then the rod came into the hands of Abraham, then of Isaac, then of Jacob, who supported himself upon it when he came into the land of Egypt, where he gave it to Joseph, the best beloved of his sons. After the death of Joseph, the rod was deposited in Pharaoh's treasury and from there Jethro had taken it when he departed from the land of Egypt and went to the land of Midian. One day, when he was walking in his garden in Midian, Jethro, without thinking, struck the earth with the rod. Suddenly the rod took root in the soil and became a tree which produced fruits.

Moses asked Zipporah, "Where is this tree?" He proceeded to the garden and pulled up the tree. Immediately the tree became a rod again having the color of sapphire, which it had from heaven, and having graven upon its top the name of the Holy One, blessèd be he, that none here below had as yet uttered.

Then Jethro thought in his heart, "This man is surely one of the sons of that Abraham through whom so many blessings are to come to the world." He embraced Moses and said to him, "Take my daughter; be my son. But swear that you will never do as Jacob your ancestor did who, having married the daughters of Laban, one day fled again from Laban's house."

Moses swore to it and became the spouse of Zipporah. She bore him a son whom he named Gershom, *A Stranger There,* saying, "I was a stranger there and there was I blessed."

Now, say our teachers, if Maror had not coveted Shelomith, if Dathan had not betrayed Moses, Moses would never have fled to the land of Midian and he would never have known there what God wanted of him. But Maror coveted Shelomith, Dathan betrayed Moses and Moses fled to the land of Midian and there knew what God wanted of him. Thus the instinct of evil, without wishing it, did the will of the Eternal.

CHAPTER V

THE FAITHFUL SHEPHERD

Moses pastured Jethro's flocks, watching over them lovingly. First he led the beasts that were youngest forth to pasture so they could feed upon the tender grasses, then the older beasts who found a stronger herbage and last the most vigorous who browsed upon the toughest forage. Then said God, "He has learned how to shepherd sheep, giving to each his sustenance; he will learn how to shepherd my people, giving to everyone their rights."

One day a kid escaped from the flock. Moses hurried after it and found it in a rocky place drinking at a spring. "Poor kid," he said to it, "You fled in order to drink? Surely you are weary," and taking it on his shoulder, he brought it back to the flock.

Then God said, "Since he has had pity upon a poor kid, bearing it upon his shoulder to take upon him its weariness. Then will he have pity upon my poor people, bearing them in his heart to take upon him their sin."

For God, before entrusting the flocks of people to his rulers and prophets, entrusts to them, to try them, the flocks of his beasts.

The bondage of Egypt weighed more heavily each day upon the children of Israel. Pharaoh, angered at knowing Moses was their brother, punished them for his past mistake. To bring him to repentance, God sent Pharaoh a sickness of leprosy. From the crown of his head to the soles of his feet he was covered with pustules. But he did not know how to read in his suffering the message of the Most High and instead of his soul, he sought to heal his body.

Every morning, for ten years, he had ten Hebrew children torn from the arms of the mothers of Israel and every morning for ten years he bathed in their blood. But neither his soul nor his body were healed. When he died he could not be embalmed; his skin fell away in filth and his stench rotted the unguents.

The Pharaoh who came after him was the son of that Bithiah who had saved Moses from the waters. She, being cured of her barrenness, had conceived this firstborn of her flesh after Moses, the firstborn of her spirit, fled to Jethro. Yet despite her prayers, the new Pharaoh was even crueler than the old, for no leprosy tormented him; his only torment was his cruelty. Every evening at his meat he threw ten of the Hebrew children to his dogs and while he ate, he looked upon his dogs as they devoured them.

Then the cry of the mothers rose up to God—not that the Israelites deserved to be saved, for their sins were countless, but the Lord remembered his promise to the Patriarchs and wished that from this people's infamy there should be born for all peoples a blessing.

Amram was dead. Moses' hour had come; for, say our sages, when the sun of a righteous man goes down, at once the sun of another shines out. And the faithful shepherd, grazing Jethro's flocks, went farther into the desert each day. A force drew him there—he sought the presence of God. To receive in oneself the presence of God, one must make within oneself a desert.

One day, in the midst of the wilderness, he saw a mountain of granite and of sapphire. As he went toward it, it came toward him. This mountain is called by several names: by the name of *Hatred*, Sinai, for from it came down hatred of sin; by the name of the *Sword*, Horeb, for from it came down the sword of justice; by the name of the *Advent,* Bâ-sham, for upon it came the Lord.

When Moses stopped at the foot of the mountain, the mountain likewise stopped. Then he beheld a bush of thorns and in the bush, a fire; the fire burned, yet the bush was not consumed. And in this bush of thorns the presence of God appeared to him.

Why in a bush of thorns? ask our doctors.

Rabbi Eliezer answers, "Because the thornbush is the humblest of trees, and Israel the humblest of peoples."

Rabbi Johanan replies, "Because the thornbush is the hedge of gardens, and Israel is the hedge of the world."

Rabbi Joshua replies, "Because the thornbush is the dolorous tree and God suffers when the children of Israel suffer."

And why did the fire burn within the bush and yet the bush itself was not consumed?

Rabbi Nahman replies, "Because grief is in Israel, but God does not wish it to consume Israel."

Moses was not yet a prophet, so he could not yet hear God's voice. If the Eternal had spoken with his voice of thunder, Moses would have been terrified; if he had spoken in his still small voice, Moses would not have heard him. So what did God do? To speak to Moses he took the voice of Amram, Moses' father, calling him, "Moses, Moses!"

Moses answered, "What do you want, my father? Here am I."

"I am not your father," said God. "I am the God of your father, the God of Abraham, of Isaac and of Jacob."

Moses rejoiced in his heart, thinking, "God sets my father among the Patriarchs and even before the Patriarchs!" But, fearing to behold the Lord, he covered his face.

Upon this point Rabbi Joshua bar Karha and Rabbi Hosea were not of the same opinion. The first said, "Moses did wrong to hide his face, for if he had not hidden it God would have shown him, then and there, what is on high and what is below, what has been and what is to be."

The second said, "Moses did well to hide his face for God said to him, 'Since you honor me by hiding your face, upon my life I will speak to you face-to-face all your life long.' "

In truth, whereas he spoke to the other prophets only in certain hours and through veils or mirrors, the Lord from that hour forth conversed with Moses in every hour, speaking to him face-to-face.

God continued, "The cry of the children of Israel has reached me and I have also seen the oppression wherewith the Egyptians oppress them. Now therefore go. I send you unto Pharaoh. Bring forth my people out of Egypt and lead them unto this mountain where they shall know me and into that country flowing with milk and honey which I promised to their ancestors."

But Moses could not find in his heart the courage to obey and for seven days he resisted the will of the Eternal.

The first day he said, "Lord, who am I, to bring forth your children of Israel? I am only a shepherd lost in the wilderness."

God answered, "The weaker the person whom I use, the more that person reveals my strength."

The second day Moses said, "Lord, you are sending me to your enemies. They have sought my life; they seek it yet."

God answered, "He with whom I go, my fear goes with him."

The third day Moses said, "I, your servant, hesitate to obey you. How then shall Pharaoh obey me? I am slow of speech and have a slow tongue. Where shall I dare to find words to speak to him?"

God answered, "Did Adam know how to speak when he gave names to all the beasts of the field? Who, then, made him speak? I open the eyes of them who see and I close the eyes of them who see not. To those who hear I give hearing and from those who hear not I take hearing away. I have made the mouth from whence comes the word; you will speak if my word is in your mouth."

The fourth day Moses said, "You have sworn to their ancestors to save their children and now you would have me save them! To save Lot, who was but a man, you sent an angel; to save Hagar, who was but a woman, you sent an angel. Yet would you have me, who am but a man and more cowardly than woman or child, to save a whole people! O Lord, save them yourself, or else send your angel, or if you must have a person, send your Messiah, the Messiah of your peace and justice!"

God answered, "He shall come in the end of days; you are his beginning. Assuredly I could save them out of Egypt on the four wheels of my heavenly chariot, or bear them away on the wings of my seraphim who are myriads upon myriads. But it is you that they await and that I await. It is in your hands. If you do not accomplish it, it shall not be accomplished. I would that you should wish this thing, but I will not constrain you: all must work with God to accomplish God's work."

The fifth day Moses said, "Lord, Lord, do they deserve salvation? Are they not defiled with sin?"

And God answered, "Put your hand into your bosom and then take it out."

He put in his hand and took it out: it was leprous.

"Put it into your bosom again and then pluck it out."

He did it and his hand was purified.

God said again, "As I can take away the leprosy from your hand, so can I take away their sin from their souls."

The sixth day Moses said, "But how am I to feed them on the long march? Where shall I find food and drink for a whole people? They have no provision but tears and lamentation and the road that leads unto you goes through a desert."

God answered, "Was there wheat when there was no earth? When the heavens were not, was there water? The One who brought forth from the void heaven and earth can bring forth from the desert water and bread."

The seventh day Moses said, "But if I follow you, will they follow me, O Lord? Will they believe me, if I believe you? Give me a sign, so that they shall follow me; tell me your name, that they may believe me."

And God answered, "My names are numberless as my powers. In my might I am called Sabaoth; in my long-suffering, El Shaddai; in my justice, Elohim; in my mercy, Adonai. But look on the four unutterable signs I have engraved on your rod of sapphire. They contain the name that contains all my names and my powers which signify, I AM THAT I AM.[1] Go, say unto the children of Israel, I AM is with me."

Then Moses arose and desired to go. But see how faithful to his word was the faithful shepherd: even while he accomplished God's command, he remembered his promise to Jethro and did not leave him the way Jacob had fled Laban. He said to him, "Give me my wife and my two sons so I may go to deliver the Hebrews."

Jethro answered, "Would you have three slaves more to deliver? Leave your wife and your sons. Go in peace to your people and in peace return again."

And Moses went forth alone, riding upon an ass. According to our doctors this same ass had borne the wood of the burnt offering when our father Abraham went to Moriah to offer up Isaac and this same ass shall bear the Messiah when he shall come upon the world in the End of Days.

[1] Literally, in French and in Hebrew, *I Am He Who Is.*

CHAPTER VI

THE ROD OF SAPPHIRE

When the Lord had spoken to Moses his voice had divided into two voices—while one said to him in the burning bush, "Rise up from the wilderness and go into Egypt," the other spoke to Aaron in the bondage of Goshen, saying, "Rise up from Egypt and go into the wilderness."

Each obedient, they met on the way and embraced. It is for this that it is written: *Mercy and truth meet, justice and peace embrace.* For Moses was truth and Aaron was mercy; Aaron brought peace and Moses justice. Moses that day was four score years old and Aaron on that day four score and three.

The faithful shepherd told his brother what God wanted of them: they came to Goshen and assembled the Elders of Israel and told them the matter. Then a cry went up from their bondage, "Save us, Moses, save us!"

The one who made bricks cried to him and the one who dug trenches; the one who bore the straw cried and the one who bore the stone; the one who was building houses and the one who was building cities; and, next the rotting dead, the dying also cried, "Save us! Save us!" And they thought, "This god of whom they spoke to us and whom we saw not ... if he *were* God? ... Perchance he is sending us a savior." And faith was born in their hearts.

For Israel, our sages say, is like the olive: when ripe on the tree, it is taken away and carried to the press and put under the mill and milled and bound with ropes and loaded with stones.

Then it gives forth oil. Likewise with the children of Israel: the peoples of the earth take them, then they strike them, then they fasten upon them chains and yokes and stifle them in their prisons and crush them beneath their feet. Then Israel gives forth, like precious oil, its prayer to God.

But the Israelites were not all slaves. Some added acre to acre, harvest to harvest, traded in copper, in jewels, in porphyry. At ease in their gardens of tumbling waters, in their halls where idols were painted upon the walls, they had for friends the sons of Egypt. Like them they went barefoot and bare-shouldered with painted skin, and like them they called themselves, instead of Phanuel, Peniel or Osiel, Meti, Teti, or Atoti.

The richest of all, Korah, son of Izhar, of the family of Kohath, called himself Koracti to the Egyptians. Great was his name over Egypt, for he was Pharaoh's treasurer, as once Joseph had been, and he kept all the keys of all his treasures.

But his riches were not a gift of the Holy One, blessèd be he, as Joseph's before him; for Joseph stored up for all, but Korah for himself alone. When Joseph passed by, the daughters of kings threw rings and necklaces to him from their windows, but when Korah passed by, the children of the poor turned in the street to spit upon him.

Now when they heard Moses' intention and the hope of their brethren, these Hebrews whose hearts were with Egypt were filled with great fear. They thought, "If Pharaoh would keep his Hebrew slaves, perhaps his anger will turn against us, and if he would let them go, perhaps he will banish us with them."

So Korah sent Dathan as his envoy among the slaves of Goshen who whispered into their ears, "Why therefore would you depart? Korah is mighty over Pharaoh's might: he will lighten your bondage."

And the children of Israel said one to another, "Why therefore should we depart?"

Meanwhile for seven days the Elders had debated whether or not they would follow Moses toward the Promised Land. Some said, "Remember Ganon, son of Eran, who desired to lead thither the sons of Ephraim 40 years ago? Where did they arrive? Their bones rot in the wilderness."

Others answered them, "They did not have a man sent from God as a guide."

One said, "How should Moses save us? I have computed, according to the prophecies, the days and the months and the years: the time is not come."

Another answered, "How should he not save us? I have computed, according to the prophecies, the years and the months and the days: the time is come."

After a week Pagiel the son of Ocran, of the tribe of Asher, came saying, "Jacob, as he died, whispered to Joseph his son the secret of the sign which the savior shall bear: Joseph, as he died, whispered it to his brethren; Asher, the last of the brethren, as he died whispered it into the ear of Serah, my mother; my mother is 200 years old and she is about to die. Come and let Serah my mother reveal to the Elders the secret of the sign, before she dies."

They came. In her clay hut, upon her bed of pain, Serah was already giving up the ghost; her dead eyes could no more see and her dead mouth whispered, "A rod ... of sapphire ... and upon the rod ... a name ... graven. ... And this name ..."

She said no more. The 70 Elders looked upon Moses. In his hand he held the rod and on the rod was the name. Then they said, "Let Moses and Aaron lead us. With them we will all speak before Pharaoh's face." And they went up, Moses and Aaron going before, the 70 Elders going after.

Pharaoh's palace had 100 gates and before each gate an army. When they saw these gates and the 100 armies, 20 of the Elders trembled and fled.

Pharaoh's palace also had 100 courts and in each court a lion; when they saw the courts and the 100 lions, 26 of the Elders groaned and fled.

In Pharaoh's hall was Pharaoh. When they saw Pharaoh, the 24 who remained paled and fled.

It was for this, our doctors comment, that when Moses and Aaron went up into Sinai, God forbade the Elders to follow them.

That day Pharaoh happened to be celebrating the anniversary of his sovereignty. All the kings of the earth had come and, prostrate, had set their crowns beneath his feet, crying, "You are god over all the earth."

Moses and Aaron said to Pharaoh, "Thus saith the Lord God of Israel: 'Let my people go, that they may hold a feast unto me in the wilderness.' "

"Since when have slaves had a god?" Pharaoh answered. "The Eternal, you say? I know not this god." Turning to his 70 scribes who knew the 70 tongues of earth, he asked them, "Do you know a god who is called the Eternal?"

They answered, "We have sought in all the books written in all the languages the names of all the gods: the Eternal is not God."

"You sought him among the dead," Moses and Aaron answered. "Our God is a living God."

"How old is he?" asked Pharaoh. "How long has he reigned? What cities has he conquered? What lands has he subdued?"

Moses and Aaron answered, "Before the world, He Was; after the world, he shall reign. When he goeth in mercy, mercy is his girdle and love is his crown. But when he goeth in justice, fire is his bow, flame is his arrow; the clouds are his buckler, the lightning his sword; the sky is his chariot's canopy, the earth is its pavement."

"If he is almighty," said Pharaoh, "let him give a sign of his might."

Then Aaron, taking the rod of sapphire from Moses' hands, threw it on the ground and it was changed into a serpent.

Why into a serpent? our rabbis ask. Because the serpent, like Pharaoh, had blasphemed the Lord God.

But when he saw the serpent, Pharaoh laughed a great laugh, saying, "You would teach magic unto the Egyptians? If those are the miracles of your God, the littlest children of my littlest sorcerers can do as much."

And in truth, out of ten parts of sorcery that the world has received, nine have been received by Egypt. Jannesh and Jambresh, the two sons of Balaam who were Pharaoh's two greatest magicians, summoned all the children of the magicians and they cast down upon the ground all their rods, which all became serpents. But Aaron's serpent swallowed up all the other serpents.

Then Pharaoh, his nostrils swollen with his rage, cried out, "Slaves! You would invent a god to free yourselves from bondage? I will teach you that the god of heaven and earth, it is I."

But the Eternal said, "You shall come to know him, this God whom you know not."

To punish the Hebrews, Pharaoh ordered that every man should make double the quantity of bricks each day from then on. In the evening if a brick should be lacking, a child was to be torn from a mother in Israel to replace the brick. Thus the men of Israel who were building houses and cities had, in place of the missing bricks, to cover up with lime their children, with all their tears and weeping, and bury them alive in the walls.

Dathan, Korah's envoy, whispered into the ears of the Israelites, "You see how Moses saves you! State that you do not want to depart and Korah shall save you."

So the Israelites said to Moses, "Let Korah protect us: we no longer want to depart."

Then Moses cried out to the Eternal, "Alas, Lord, you did say to me that you were a God merciful and long-suffering and that you would fulfil through me your promise to the Patriarchs. I had scarcely spoken your name in front of Pharaoh before a greater evil has come upon your people."

God answered, "Alas, Moses, that my Patriarchs are no more upon earth! They did not ask my name before they served me. I said to Abraham: 'I will give you this land of my choice.' Yet when he went to bury Sarah there, he still possessed no land and needs must purchase a burial plot. Yet he complained not unto me. I said to Isaac: 'I will give you this land of my choice.' Yet when he needed water there, he had to strive with the herdsmen of Gerar. Yet he complained not unto me. I said to Jacob: 'I will give you this land of my choice.' Yet when he had to abandon it because of Esau's hatred, he complained not unto me.

"But as for you—I have told you my name that holds all my power and, at the first trial, you lament. Were I Justice only, I would punish you. I am Mercy, I forgive you. Go now. I send you unto Pharaoh to enlighten him by my wonders. However stiff-necked he may be, respect him as the king and depart not with my people until he shall permit it unto you.

"I send you unto Israel to save my people by my wonders. However sinful they be, respect the people and condemn them not save when their sin shall exceed my long-suffering."

Then, to enlighten Pharaoh and to save the children of Israel, the Holy One, blessèd be he, sent upon Egypt ten plagues.

CHAPTER VII

THE TEN PLAGUES

It is written: *I will multiply my wonders.* Of this our sages have said, "The Lord is a Lord of hosts."

Now what does a lord of hosts do when he would reduce his enemies? He surrounds their citadel and cuts off their supply of water. If they surrender, all is well; if not, he brings up his trumpets, which terrify them with their clamor. If they surrender, all is well; if not, he brings up his bowmen, who let fly their arrows. If they surrender, all is well; if not, he brings up his cohorts of every nation to show his might; he slaughters their flocks, he pours boiling oil upon them, he hurls upon them balls of stone, he scales their walls, he imprisons them in their dungeons. If they surrender, all is well; if not, he massacres their chieftains.

And that is what the Lord did to the Egyptians. First he deprived them of water by changing the Nile into blood: they refused to let the Israelites go. Then he sent them the croaking frogs: they refused to let the Israelites go. Then he sent upon them the lice which pierced them with their stings: but they refused to let the Israelites go. He sent upon them flies of every kind: still they refused. He sent upon them the plague on their livestock: still they refused. He sent upon them the plague of festering boils, the plague of hail that smote them with its hailstones, the locusts that climbed upon them as upon ladders: and still they refused. He sent them the darkness that imprisoned them in dungeons: they refused to let the Israelites go. Then he slew their firstborn.

See how the man of war differs from the God of war? The man of war who wants to destroy his enemy, attacks him by surprise; he does not space out his blows and when he has the enemy beneath his feet, he makes an end of him. But God warned Pharaoh ten times and ten times gave him an opportunity to repent. Before punishing him, ten times God showed Pharaoh mercy.

Why, asks Rabbi Tanhuma, was it Aaron and not Moses who upon God's command, struck the river, then the shore, changing the water into blood and into frogs and then the sand into lice? It was because the sand had saved Moses before by hiding the Egyptian whom Moses had slain. It was because the water had saved Moses before by bearing his cradle. Could Moses have struck his saviours, the sand and the water?

When the river was turned to blood, all the waters in all Egypt were turned into blood: the water in lakes and in springs and in pools; the water in leather bottles and in pitchers and in goblets. When an Egyptian spit, his very spittle was blood. But whenever an Israelite drew or poured water, it was still water. What then did the Israelites do whose hearts were with Egypt? They sold water to the Egyptians.

When the frogs came up from the river, one came up first, alone, and began to croak. At his call all the others appeared and covered the entire land of Egypt. Did a drop of water fall upon a grain of sand? Croaking, a frog came forth from it. Did a drop of spittle fall from an opened mouth? Croaking, a frog came forth from it. Croaking, they swarmed into the fields and the gardens, into the cellars and the barns, into the wine presses and the kneading-troughs. They swarmed over the statues, the markets, the pyramids, the open places. When the porphyry portals of a palace stayed their march, they said, croaking to the portals, "Let us pass, that we may do the will of our Creator." Then the portals opened and the frogs entered, climbed up the painted walls and jumped, croaking, upon the ivory beds and into the golden vessels from which the princes of the Egyptians ate. At the frontier of Goshen the croaking frogs became silent and the Israelites in Goshen thought, "Could Korah work such a wonder?"

The magicians of Egypt, imitating Aaron's miracles, had like him turned water into blood, then into frogs; but when he turned sand into lice and made of all Egypt an unsealed tomb wherein the worms awaited the Egyptians, Pharaoh's magicians could still turn the dust into lice, but not the lice back into dust. Then Pharaoh said to Moses, "Let this plague cease; entreat your God and I will let the Israelites go to sacrifice to him in the wilderness."

They entreated God; the plague ceased. But Pharaoh did not keep his word. "Return in seven days," he said. "I will keep your women and children as hostages." For, our sages comment, he was like those sinners who cry to the Lord God in their distress, but deny him as soon as his compassion has wearied of trying them.

Then, warning him each time and each time finding his heart yet more hardened, Moses sent the flies and the plague on livestock and the festering boils.

Why flies of every kind? asks Rabbi Jehudah. Because, but for Moses, idolaters of every race would have covered up Israel. Why the plague on livestock? Because, but for Moses, the cow and the ox, the goat and the lamb—the idols of the Egyptians—would have remained the gods of Israel. And why the festering boils? Because, but for Moses, idolatry, like an ulcer, would have eaten up Israel.

And when the flies were over Egypt, every clod of earth, every stone, every blade of grass, every leaf of every tree was a moving army of flies and of ants, of fleas and of bugs, of cockroaches and of wood lice.

All the walls, all the roofs, all the ramparts of all the cities seemed but one surging mass. Men and women, the young and the old, beggars and princes alike were clothed from head to foot in the fetid swarming. Then Pharaoh summoned Korah and the Israelites whose hearts were with Egypt—who along with those in Goshen had been spared—and said to them, "Are you Egyptians or are you Hebrews? Choose. Where did this plague come from? Your brethren! Let it cease or I will drive you forth with them."

When the plague came upon the livestock, the sheep grazing burst within their fleeces; the udders of the smothered cows gave forth bile; the carcasses of the oxen encumbered the fields. And in the temples where the painted priests offered up to them sacrifices, Hapi, the ox and Hathor, the cow, dissolved in corruption. The Egyptians wept at the death of their gods. Then Korah, with the Israelites whose hearts were with Egypt, came and chided Moses, crying, "When will you stop overwhelming Pharaoh, *our* brother? Must we leave our country for a rabble of slaves?"

When the vile boils had made a festering sore of every foot and every thigh, every back and breast, every neck and face, the Israelites, whose bodies stayed spotless, thought, "If it be a God who protects us, ought not our souls also to be purified before him?"

But the Lord, perceiving that Pharaoh hardened his heart, hardened it yet more. Then came the hail, stoning the Egyptians. Then the locusts, devouring them. Then the darkness.

In this darkness the one who had lain down could not find room to stand up and the one who was standing could not find a place to lie down for the darkness was thick and hard as metal, coming from hell. Nor could any speak or hear or eat or drink, as it blinded their eyes, it blinded their mouths and their ears. And they starved, motionless in the blackness. But among the children of Israel there shone great lights for they were already illumined by the splendor of the Eternal.

To Pharaoh alone of all Egypt God had left a voice, to repent for all. This voice cried out in the darkness, "Moses! Entreat your God. Let the day return and you shall go!"

Moses prayed and the day returned. And many among the Egyptians said, "These Hebrews are mighty: a God is with them." What did the Israelites whose hearts were with Egypt do then? They borrowed from them vessels of gold and silver, thinking within their hearts, "If we are to go, let us not go with empty hands; the labor of 603,000 slaves during 430 years is indeed worthy of a small wage."

Korah, fearing he would be driven out with the others, wished to take with him all the riches of Egypt. Now Joseph, foreseeing a time of trial for his lord, had buried an immense treasure of gems and jade, of ivory, of gold dust near the river, beneath an obelisk—for in the days of the famine all the peoples of the earth had come to buy his corn. Korah knew the place where the treasure lay: he had forced the secret from the aged Serah, the last descendant of Joseph's last brother. So one night hundreds of Korah's slaves, binding ropes about the obelisk, overthrew it and raising a slab of basalt found a key so heavy that 30 mules would not have been able to carry it. They opened the cave and entered by the light of a torch. As they came out one by one, their backs were bowed beneath the ingots which they piled into their chariots. Upon the other bank of the river in the light of a single torch, all alone, stood Moses.

A voice from God had guided him to the secret place where Joseph was buried. The Egyptians, knowing that his embalmed body would be a blessing upon their land, had desired that no one should ever be able to tear him from his tomb. Thus they had turned aside the river's channel and digging in the depths a deep trench, had there laid to rest the sacred body in a coffin of porphyry. For centuries the Nile, ever overflowing and returning within its banks, had rolled its sustenance-giving waves over the remains of this dead Israelite. Now Joseph, when he lay dying, had said to his brother, "It is known to me that a time shall come when the Egyptians in their ungratefulness shall put upon you a heavy bondage. But with strong hand and mighty arm the Lord shall bring you out of this land into the land of your ancestors. Then carry up my bones from here and have a sepulchre hewn for me in the one land where the dry bones shall live again, wherein the dead shall see God."

So Moses had come and holding his torch's flame over the water he called, "Joseph! Joseph! The hour is come! God waits but for you! We go! Come with us!"

The waters boiled in the depths and guided by an invisible hand the dripping porphyry of the coffin came to rest upon the prophet's back. So while on the one bank of the river Korah bore away in the procession of his chariots Joseph's riches, on the other Moses bore away his holiness.

Then God said to Moses, "This Joseph whom you carry into the land of his ancestors, carried his father Jacob into the land of his ancestors to bury him, yet it was but his duty as a son. Joseph was not a father to you; you have no duty to him to bury him. Thus the Lord, who has no duty to his creatures, shall himself bury you." So it is written: *The Lord buried Moses in the valley.*

Yet once more Pharaoh broke his word. Scarcely had he found the sun again before he again planned to sin. "Go with your women," he said to the Hebrews. "I will keep your little ones."

Moses answered, "Wretched sinner, do you think our God, instead of striking flocks, could not have struck you and blotted you from the world? But he would have you save yourself with us. Let us go, young and old, father and son, mothers and babes. Instead of keeping back, come and bring offerings for the Lord."

"Give up the labor of 600,000 slaves," Pharaoh cried, "and give them gifts as well? Get away from me; let me see your face no more!" And Moses said, "You shall see it no more; for thus saith the Lord God of Israel: 'If you do not repent and let my people go, I will count six nights; and on the seventh night about midnight will I go out into the midst of Egypt: and all the firstborn in the land of Egypt shall die, from the firstborn of Pharaoh that sitteth upon the throne, even unto the firstborn of the maidservant that is behind the mill.' "

Why the firstborn? Rabbi Tanhuma asks. Because the Egyptians had drowned the newborn of Israel and because Israel is the first-born of the Lord.

It was in the month of Nisan, which is the first month. In this month Abraham had received the blessing of the Holy One, blessèd be he; in this month Isaac had received the blessing of the Holy One, blessèd be he; in this month Jacob had received the blessing of the Holy One, blessèd be he. And when the night that the Lord had said was near, the Israelites entreated Moses, saying, "How shall God save us, for our sins are without number?"

He answered, "Renew in your flesh the covenant of the Patri-archs." For except for those of the tribe of Levi, none among them was circumcised.

When they had circumcised their flesh, Moses said to them, "The Lord our God has sent the plague on the livestock upon the animals that are the idols of the Egyptians and that were your idols; now therefore you shall sacrifice a beast of your flocks that was your idol and the Egyptians'. And you shall take a lamb, one for each family, a lamb without blemish, a male of the first year; you shall mingle its blood with the blood of the circumcision; then you shall take a bunch of hyssop [for, say our rabbis, God wished to show through hyssop, which is the least of herbs, his greatness, which is the greatest of greatnesses] ; you shall dip it in this mingled blood and you shall strike it on the two side-posts of the door in memory of Isaac and of Jacob and on the lintel in memory of Abraham.

"Then you shall roast the whole lamb with fire and shall eat it with your loins girded, your shoes on your feet and your staff in your hand. You shall eat it in haste, praising the Lord with the bitter herbs of bondage and the bread of freedom, without leaven. Let no one go out before the dawn, for in this night the Lord will smite all the firstborn of Egypt and against all the gods of Egypt he will execute judgment. But he will see upon your houses the blood of the covenant and the blood of the Passover that shall deliver you from Egypt and from all the idols of the Egyptians.

"The Lord will pass over you and will not destroy you. Thus this night shall be for you a memorial and you shall keep it a feast to the Lord throughout your generations; you shall keep it with a feast, you and your children and your children's children, unto the Passover when the Messiah shall feast over the whole world."

When every one of the children of Israel had roasted the lamb with fire, God summoned the four winds that blow from Eden and commanded them, saying, "Blow toward the west, toward the east, toward the south, toward the north."

They blew and the fragrance of the Passover spread over all the earth. Then the kings of the earth asked, "What is this fragrance?"

And the angels of heaven answered, "It is Israel, who is preparing the salvation of the world."

While this passed, many of the righteous among the firstborn of the Egyptians had fled to the children of Israel and the children of Israel had welcomed them, for it is written: *This is the gateway of the Lord, the Righteous shall enter in*—not only the righteous in Israel, but all that are righteous in the eyes of the Eternal.

And many of the wicked among the firstborn of the Egyptians had fled to the temples of their idols. But there they were in no way saved, for the will of God is fulfilled.

And it came to pass that at midnight the Lord of hosts, the unbeheld Sabaoth, came down upon Egypt with 9,000 myriads of destroying angels of whom some were of invisible iron and others of fire invisible. But when the angels of iron and of fire would have hurled upon the Egyptians their fire and their iron, God stayed them, saying, "Justice is the Lord's alone."

Then there was a great cry in Egypt for there was no house where there was not one dead. Dead were the firstborn of their sons, dead the firstborn of their daughters, dead the firstborn of their princes, dead the firstborn of their vassals, the firstborn of the rich and of the poor, even to the firstborn of the captives in the dungeons who had said, "We would rather remain captives than see Israel delivered," and those of the slaves who grinding the corn between the millstones had said, "We would rather remain slaves than see Israel set free." Dead even the firstborn of the dead, for the dogs nosed them out in their tombs to make them die a second death. And over all the earth all the idols of all the nations died also—those of stone dissolved into dust, those of wood into corruption and those of metal into watery stench.

That night Pharaoh in his palace did not wait for his slaves to awake him. He was wakened by the universal cry. And when he had risen, alone and without help in the night, his foot stumbled. his hand felt about in the dark. Upon the dais of porphyry there lay his son, stricken dead.

Then tumult went all about the palace. It entered by the 100 gates and filled the 100 courts and sonorous halls and resounding walls. All the mothers, all the fathers, all the people gathered in anguish and trembling, crying out to their king, "Let them go or we shall all be dead!" But he answered them not, for, say our sages, when the sinner has been nine times tried and nine times has refused to repent, God refuses the sinner the desire to repent.

A forest of arms rose up, a forest of clenched hands stretched out toward him; whips and rods, spears and swords circled with threatening death the silent face of Pharaoh. Suddenly the uplifted arms, the clenched fists, the rods and whips, the swords and spears circling that silent face were stilled: a distant scraping was heard. Beneath a green aura the scraping drew nearer in the silence of the night. Along the river and through the gardens, by the sphinxes and the pylons, the scraping luminosity drew nearer—below the aura a mask with painted eyes, below the mask, swathings and below the swathings, two motionless feet, that walked.

All knew that it was Bithiah's mummy come from its pyramid: Bithiah, mother of Pharaoh in the flesh, mother of Moses in the spirit. A hand came forth from the swathing and took Pharaoh's hand—the mother led away her son into the silence of the night.

Together they went toward a light; together they went toward singing. When they had come to a door whose side-posts and lintel were stained with blood, dead Bithiah knocked: the door opened. Living Pharaoh saw Hebrews who were singing standing all about a smoking meat, their loins girded, their shoes upon their feet and their staffs in their hands.

Then he cried out, "Moses!"

A voice answered, "You shall see me no more."

Again he cried out, "I have sinned, Moses, I have sinned. I know him now, the God whom I knew not. I bring you all my crowns for him. Go in peace and bless me also!"

And behind him all the mothers, all the fathers, all the people cried out, "We offer up all our riches unto the Lord God: go in peace and bless us also."

But the voice said again, "Ye shall see me no more."

Then the breath of dead Bithiah murmured, "Moses, my son, for the sake of her who saved you, will you not save the firstborn of my flesh? you who are the firstborn of my spirit?"

And Moses answered, "Mother who did save me, for your sake I would have sought to save all Egypt. Why were you not there to save it with me?"

Showing his face to Pharaoh, Moses asked, "Is it your will to say after me in a loud voice the words I shall say to you?"

"It is my will."

"Then repeat: 'Children of Israel, be free. You were my slaves, now you are the servants of the Lord.' "

Pharaoh said it; all those who were there heard his voice. "Say it a second time," said Moses. A second time he repeated it: and all Egypt heard his voice. "A third time say it."

And a third time he said, "Children of Israel, be free; you were my slaves, now you are the servants of the Lord."

And the whole world heard his voice. Then Bithiah returned to her shadows and, as if a thousand suns together had suddenly shone forth, day appeared; for, say our rabbis, the children of Israel were not to flee in the night, like slaves, but to go forth freed, in the full light of day. Fathers and sons, mothers and daughters, the young and the old, they went forth, laden with the gifts of Egypt. Korah, Abiram, Dathan and many Israelites whose hearts were with Egypt remained with the Egyptians, but many Egyptians whose hearts were with Israel followed the Israelites.

It was the 15th day of the month of Nisan. Our doctors say that in the Appointed Time when the children of Israel shall have passed through all their captivities, on this same day of this same month the Prophet of the Wilderness shall return from the Wilderness, the Prophet of Rome shall return from Rome and the Messiah, delivering the world, shall bring peace between them and shall lead them, each leading his flock, to the Justice of Zion and to the Peace of Jerusalem.

CHAPTER VIII

"AND THE WATERS WERE DIVIDED"

The children of Israel journeyed and the Lord went before them, as it is written, in a pillar of cloud by day and in a pillar of fire by night. They journeyed toward Succoth by the eastern road that leads into the desert.

Why, asks Rabbi Joshua ben Levi, did they not take the Gath road that goes toward the north? They would have reached the Promised Land in eleven days instead of wandering 40 years in the wilderness. It is like that king who, having a son, wished to give him his inheritance, but he thought, "My son is young: he hardly knows how to read and write. If I give him all my possessions now, will he be able to keep them? I will wait until he has grown in strength and wisdom." In the same way God thought, "The children of Israel are verily still children: first let me teach them to understand and practice my law. When they have grown to adulthood in my precepts and my commandments, then will I give them the Promised Land."

Now as soon as they had gone forth, Pharaoh regretted letting them go. Rabbi Simeon ben Levi says it is like that man who had a garden and sold it to his neighbor, not knowing what his garden contained.

"How much did you sell it for?" he was asked.

"A hundred ribous."

"But in your garden there were vines worth 10,000 ribous, olive trees worth 10,000, pomegranates worth 10,000 and trees of spice worth 10,000."

Then the man regretted what he had done.

Likewise Pharaoh. When the children of Israel had fled, the chief men of the Egyptians came to him and said, "Look what you have lost! Did you not know how many artisans there were in Israel and how many rich men and how many wise ones?"

Then Pharaoh regretted what he had done.

Instantly he called out his army. He himself, in his haste, harnessed his own chariot. All the chief men of the Egyptians did like him. Instead of two horses, he harnessed three. All the warriors of the Egyptians did like him. He went so swiftly that in one day he covered the ground the children of Israel had journeyed over in three. Against each of them he brought 300 warriors and he took with him all his treasure so that he might enroll, if it were necessary, all the peoples of the earth.

Samael, the angel of death, went before him with his myriads. Korah, Dathan, Abiram and all the Israelites of the Court of Egypt followed him, thinking, "If Pharaoh triumphs, we will stay with Pharaoh. If he is vanquished by God, we will go with God."

Moses, unwilling to flee before the might of man, had brought Israel from Etham to Pi-hahiroth, by Baal-Zephon at the shores of the sea. There, hewn from the rock, was the one idol in the universe that the Lord, to give Pharaoh confidence and so better to ensure his ruin, had allowed to remain standing. All the beasts of the desert came out against the children of Israel. Pharaoh, learning this, rejoiced, saying, "Baal-Zephon protects me: he will give me victory."

When the children of Israel saw the sea before them, the beasts of the desert on the right, and on the left and behind them all Egypt in arms, they were stricken with terror and cried out to Moses, "What have you done? Your enemies will kill *us* because of *your* plagues. It would have been better to serve the Egyptians than to die here."

Some among the wailing women and children gathered stones to stone him. But Moses, paying no attention, answered them, "Do you think that God sent the Egyptians the rivers of blood, the frogs, the lice, the flies, the plague on livestock, the festering boils, the hail, the locusts, the darkness and the death of the firstborn only to bring death upon us now? His miracles of yesterday promise his miracles of tomorrow. Armies, wild beasts and seas are nothing before him. Believe in his power; it shall save you."

Turning toward the Lord, Moses prayed. But God said to him, "My children are in sore distress and you pray? There is a time for prayer and a time for action. In the beginning of the world, for Adam's sake, I gathered the waters into one place and the dry land into one place. Now for my people's sake, the waters must be divided and the dry land must appear in the midst of the waters."

But Satan, wholly unwilling that Israel should be saved, appeared before the Lord and said, "Only yesterday these children of Israel adored idols and today for their sake you would divide the waters?"

What then did God do? inquire our sages. Rabbi Hama bar Hanina replies he did like that shepherd who wished to lead his sheep across the ford of a river when a wolf appeared, barring the passage. Then the shepherd took a he-goat, the strongest of the flock, and threw him to the wolf, thinking, "While the wolf is struggling with the goat I will get my sheep safely across. When they are safe, I will return and rescue the goat from him."

In the same way God, desiring to save the children of Israel from Satan, said to him, "What is the value of a few slaves' souls to you? Do you know my servant Job? His soul, by itself, is worth all theirs. You may tempt it; I abandon it to you."

He thought, "While Satan is with Job, I will save the children of Israel. When they are saved, I will retrieve Job from Satan."

Now this was that same Job, who had kept silence before Pharaoh instead of speaking with Jethro and against Balaam when he had counseled that Moses and the firstborn of Israel should be drowned in the Nile. Not having expiated his forgotten sin, he deserved chastisement, but having retired into the land of Uz between the Two Rivers in the city of his birth, he had grown rich in sons and in daughters, in oxen and in camels, in justice and in charity. Long had Satan lain in wait for this soul, precious above all others. When God had offered it to him, instantly he turned from the children of Israel and fell upon Job to torture him in heart, in spirit and in flesh.

Then the Lord said to Moses, "Stretch out your hand over the sea: it will divide and you shall pass over."

"But how can such a thing be possible?" asked the Prophet, "for did you not, in the beginning of the world, say unto the earth: 'Here is your place, you shall not depart it'?"

"Is this then the strength of your faith, Moses?" replied God. "You plead with my children, 'Believe in him,' and you yourself do not believe. Do you know whether or not in the beginning of the world I made a pact with the sea to let you pass over today? Do you think that the creation I created is finished and that someone cannot change anything in it if I consent? One of my prophets will stay the sun, whom I have commanded to journey; another will stay the rain, which I have commanded to fall; another will stay death, whom I have commanded to slay; and the last will create a new world, with a new heaven. Command the sea then to divide. If you will it, it shall divide and you shall pass over."

Moses said to the sea, "Divide!"

But the sea cried out, "I was born before you. Who are you, man born of woman, that I should obey you?"

At this reply Moses complained to God, who said, "What does a master do when a servant rebels? He strikes him. Strike then the sea with your rod: it shall open and you shall pass over."

Moses struck; the sea still resisted. Then at the right of the Prophet's right arm and the Prophet's will, the Lord stretched out his right arm and his will. Instantly a wind blew from the east—the wind that chastises the nations; the wind that blew the Deluge, that blew upon Babel, upon Sodom and upon Gomorrah, upon Jerusalem and upon Rome; the wind that in the day of Gog and Magog shall blow upon the whole earth.

All night, like the invisible shear of an invisible plow, this wind ever blowing furrowed in the midst of the waters a visible furrow. On each side the waves stood up like walls. To those on the left the archangel Gabriel cried, "Stand upright for Israel who shall bear on his left arm the holy phylactery of God's Torah." To those on the right he cried, "Stand upright for Israel, who shall receive his holy Torah from the holy right hand of God."

On the shore the twelve tribes of Israel were arguing: each claimed the glory of preceding all the others. The sons of Judah, in their anger at seeing themselves distanced, threw stones at the sons of Benjamin whose faith in God had made them run into the waves before they had divided. This holy rivalry, say our doctors, was later rewarded, for it was on the borders of Benjamin and Judah, in Solomon's Temple, that the presence of the Lord descended.

While the tribes were thus disputing in their zeal, twelve pathways separated by twelve walls of motionless crystal suddenly opened in the furrow that divided the sea and the twelve tribes marched side-by-side on these twelve paths. Suddenly Abraham, Isaac and Jacob, summoned by the mouth of the Lord from the cave of Machpelah where their bones rested, looked with their dead eyes upon his accomplished promise: translucent giants, their feet on the sand, their foreheads reaching to the heavens, they stretched out across the sea their six vast arms, whose hands, already hovering upon the further side, waited there to bless Israel's arrival.

Meanwhile, perplexed by the miracle, those Israelites whose hearts were with Egypt and whose curiosity, stronger than their fear, had drawn them beyond the vanguard of the Egyptians, debated, "There has been no battle. Is Pharaoh vanquished?" asked some.

"There has been no battle. Is Pharaoh the victor?" asked others.

"Since the sea is divided, let us go," proposed Dathan.

"But suppose it closes again, when we are in it," Abiram objected.

"Try it, in any case," Korah ordered, surrounded by his treasure.

They advanced cautiously.

Now, in order to draw on after them the Egyptians, God decided to save even the Israelites whose heart was with Egypt.

When they saw the Israelites enter into the sea, Pharaoh and his army, stupefied, at first thought them stricken with madness. When they realized that their slaves were escaping and that the road of their flight remained open, the Egyptians took up the pursuit furiously. The dried sand of the depths between the twelve walls of crystal bristled with chariots and horses, with helmets and bucklers, with javelins and pikes.

Moses, and with him God, was about to withdraw his right arm and let the waves engulf the Egyptians when Mizraim, the guardian angel of Egypt, rose up before the Lord and said, "King of the World, you are a God of Justice. Is it just that Egypt should die? Your people suffered there. Did they not also prosper? They served there. Have they not repaid themselves for their service? When they came they were 70, dying of hunger. They depart 603,000, laden with treasure. And you would put to the death those who let them come and let them go?"

The Lord replied, "Ten times I pardoned Pharaoh. Ten times he denied me. Ten times he promised my people freedom. Ten times he repudiated his promise. Now he hastens after them to make them slaves once more!"

"Lord," replied the Angel, "it is fitting that your people should be free. Where is the creature that could exist before you, if you did judge in the rigor of your Justice? Remember your Mercy, King of the World. For the eleventh time, pardon Egypt."

For the eleventh time God was about to pardon, when Michael, the guardian archangel of Israel, cried, "Look what they have done to your children!" With this he lifted up in his two flaming hands a wall wherein under the hardened lime imprisoned in the brick, all the angels saw the children of the Israelites, their agony still crying aloud.

And all the angels cried, "Behold, behold!"

Then God said, "Let my Justice reign."

The right arm of Moses, that was holding back the flood, fell and with it the right arm of the Lord. The twelve walls of crystal fled away in blinding flashes of sunlight and the sea covered up Egypt. One only escaped—Pharaoh. He became King of Nineveh. He became King of Babylon. He was called Antiochus. He was called Titus. He was called Justinian. Until the end of the world he will bear a thousand names, for, like Israel, Israel's persecutor is eternal.

While all this passed, Job, tortured by Satan, groaned out to God in the bitterness of his heart, "Does it seem good to you to overwhelm me? Why would you destroy in me the work of your hands? What have I done? What is my crime? Have I cheated the widow and the orphan or refused the laborer his wage or slammed my door against the poor or my mouth against Truth? Do you then see with the eyes of a person, you who permit the suffering of the just?"

Job did not remember his past sin. He did not know, say our rabbis, that his atonement, by turning Satan aside from Israel, served in the harmony of the world to save Israel. While he cursed his Maker, he did not hear the hymn of thanksgiving resound on the miraculous shore.

The Lord is my strength and song and he is become my salvation: He is my God, my father's God and I will exalt him. Who is like unto you, O Lord, among the gods? Who is like you, glorious in holiness, fearful in praises, doing wonders?

While this hymn of deliverance rose from earth to heaven, the angels wished to mingle their voices in it, but God said to them, "What? My children the Egyptians are dying in the sea and you would sing?"

The angels were silent, but Israel in joy completed the song:

You in your mercy have led forth the people whom you have redeemed: You guide them in your strength unto your holy habitation, to the Sanctuary, O Lord, which your hands have established. The Lord shall reign for ever and ever.

In the exaltation of this hymn the whole posterity of Abraham were filled with the breath of the Lord. For Jacob, delivered from exile, had not sung. Isaac, delivered from the knife, had not sung. Abraham, delivered from the furnace, had not sung.

On that day of the divided waters, not only Moses the prophet sang along with Miriam the prophetess, but also every man and every woman in Israel sang as did the old and the newborn. Even, in its mother's womb, the unborn child sang, for in that hour it saw more clearly the glory of the Lord than did Ezekiel, the prophet, in the hour of his exaltation.

CHAPTER IX

THE WAY OF MIRACLES

Next day, after that miraculous song which for a moment had made of Israel the very voice of God, the waves of the sea, in their rise and fall on the shore, carried to and fro in their surge the Egyptians' corpses. The children of Israel on the shore pointed out to each other their enemies, recognizing them, "*He* struck me on the back," cried one, "And *he* on the head," cried another. And they laughed in their joy.

With the corpses, the waves brought in weapons and treasure: swords, quivers, vessels, collars, emeralds, rubies. The earth said to the water, "Keep them, they are yours." To the earth, the water said, "They belong to you, take them back."

What did Abiram do then? He said to the Israelites, "Since the earth does not wish them and the sea refuses them, what if we accept them?"

They took the arrows and the javelins, the onyx and the sapphire. They put on the weapons and hid away the jewels. When Moses had the hour of departure announced, they no longer wanted to depart. Squatting on the shore, they searched for more treasure. For, say our teachers, what are humans, that God should indwell them? Soon they act like humans again and swiftly God leaves them.

Moses said to the Israelites, "Do you suppose the waters will go on casting up pearls for you until the end of the world?"

Abiram replied, "The Lord brought us out of Egypt for five things: to avenge us upon the Egyptians, to deliver up to us their treasure, to show us the way by a pillar of cloud and a pillar of fire, to open for us the sea and to hear our song. We are avenged upon the Egyptians, we have their treasure, God has divided the sea, he has led us, he has heard us. What is there left to do? Since there are no more Egyptians, let us return to Egypt?"

"Egypt," replied Moses, "you will never see again. The sea opened up for you to depart. It is closed against your return. God has delivered you to make of you his people. You will be his people at the foot of the mount."

And they went forth.

First they crossed the wilderness of Shur, which is infested by serpents so venomous that when they glide across a bird's shadow the bird dies. But the children of Israel walked upon the serpents and did not perish.

Moses said to them, "If you listen to the word of the Lord, you will live."

Then they came to Marah, where the waters are bitter.

Some murmured, "What shall we drink?"

Moses prayed and then he threw into the bitter waters a branch of bitter wood and the waters were made sweet. For, say our sages, God is not like humankind who must have sweetness to sweeten bitterness. Out of bitterness God made sweetness.

Then they came to Elim where there were twelve wells of water and 70 palm trees. But the wells gave little water and the palms little shade.

Many murmured, "What shall we drink?"

And behold the twelve wells that were scarcely able to water the 70 palm trees, produced sufficient water for the 603,000 children of Israel.

After this they came to Rephidim where there was no water.

Everyone murmured, "Have you brought us out of Egypt to kill all of us and our children and our cattle with thirst here?"

Moses said to them, "When you complain against me, you complain against God. Do you not perceive that God is trying you, as he tried the Egyptians? Will you give in to the trial, or will you prove yourselves a people worthy of the Lord?"

Then he prayed. The Lord said to him, "Take your rod, strike a rock and water will gush out."

"Is this possible?" asked the prophet. "Has not this rod brought ten plagues upon Egypt? How can it bring salvation upon Israel?

"Am I a human," replied God, "or am I God? A person wounds with a knife and heals with balm, but I, on the other hand, kill and revive with the same hand and when this hand wounds, even the wound is a healing."

Then Moses said to the children of Israel, "God has heard your complaining. This time once again he forgives you. I shall strike a rock. Water will gush out."

"He has just discovered a spring, as the shepherds do," exclaimed Dathan, "and he wants us to believe in a fresh miracle."

"Follow me," replied Moses, "you shall witness it. I will strike whatever rock you choose."

They followed him and said to him, "Strike this rock."

He struck it and the water gushed out.

But Dathan still jeered, "Must we have a miracle every day? In Egypt we had a river that flowed without ceasing. We could quench our thirst without nearly dying of it. How long will you follow this man who leads you to death, in order that you may owe your lives to him?"

Miriam, ever since the day she had entrusted Moses' cradle to the waters of the river, had believed in the miracle of the waters. Now for her sake, God worked another miracle.

On the second day of the Creation, God had created a predestined spring, the same spring where Abraham had watered his flocks after disputing it with the King of the Philistines and the same spring about which the Patriarch had prophesied. "The three score and ten generations of Israel shall water here."

When Miriam touched a sieve-like rock in the valley, that rock contained this spring. Suddenly twelve rivers gushed forth from it. Along the rivers trees were reflected, grasses and flowers gave forth fragrance. For 40 years everywhere the children of Israel journeyed in the wilderness, these twelve rivers that had gushed forth from Miriam's spring followed them. When they stopped, the rivers stopped; when they went forward, the rivers went with them. From that day on the children of Israel knew no thirst.

Before this they had ceased from all hunger. In the wilderness of Sin, after 61 meals, they realized that the provisions which they had brought out from Egypt were exhausted. They cried out against the Prophet, "In Egypt our larders were filled. Why have we come here in pursuit of starvation? Was there not room enough there in Egypt for our graves? Why did we not die there in the night of darkness, struck down by one blow like the Egyptians, rather than suffer this lingering death, that is worse than death?"

Moses replied to them, "In Egypt you were fed like haltered beasts of burden that are driven with whips. You ate the bread of bond-slaves. Will you accept no suffering, in exchange for the bread of liberty?"

Then everyone gathered stones to stone him.

Stones began flying round his head and already blood flowed from him, when Aaron and Miriam, protecting him with their own bodies, led him by force into his tent.

There he groaned to the Lord, "Behold, O Lord, what they do to your prophet. Their distress is too great for their spirit. When I try to follow your word and lead them to you, it is to murder that I lead them."

God replied to Moses, "These people act according to what they are. I shall act according to what *I* am. I will rain upon them the bread of heaven, but do not let them take more than enough for one day. Do not let them store up any for the morrow and do not let them take any on the seventh day, for in six days I created heaven and earth and on the seventh day rested, so my people, Israel, shall rest also."

When Moses reappeared before the children of Israel his countenance smiled upon them. Seeing his smile, they fell on their knees. The Prophet reported to them the Lord's word. They believed and waited.

On the next day, as it is written, in the morning the dew lay around about the camp. When the dew had disappeared, behold there on the ground of the wilderness lay something small, as small as the hoarfrost on the ground.

The children of Israel asked, "What is it?" For they did not know what it was.

Moses replied, "This is the bread which the Lord has given you to eat. Gather it, but let no one store any up for the morrow."

Now this manna contained within itself all the flavors in the world. According to Rabbi Abba, as soon as a anyone wished for a dish, the manna took on this flavor. One after the other it became meat or bread, oil or honey in the mouth.

To gather it up was an easy task, even for the most slothful, for it fell into the hands. So great was its abundance that Joshua, the son of Nun, in one morning collected enough to feed the whole assembly. It lay on the ground higher than the waters of the flood so the peoples of the east and of the west beheld God feeding his people with his heavenly bread.

And so it will be on the Day of Judgment that the wicked shall behold the righteous seated at the table of the Lord, for manna is milled in the third heaven in the mills of the angels. The saints will feed upon it in eternity.

Then they will ask God to give his blessing upon their delights and God will say to the Patriarchs, "Say the blessing for me."

The Patriarchs will say to Moses, "Say it for us; you alone are worthy."

And Moses will say it.

So each of the children of Israel gathered manna, some more and some less, but when they returned to their tents and measured it, they found that they all had sufficient for themselves and no more.

Abiram and Dathan, fearing for the morrow, kept some over. But the worms bred in it and changed it to corruption.

Moses said to them, "Will you doubt the Lord forever?"

On the eve of the Sabbath each one's share was doubled. Moses commanded the children of Israel, "Tomorrow you shall not go out, for in six days the Lord our God created heaven and earth. The seventh day, whereon God rested, shall be the day of rest of his people Israel."

That day the manna did not fall, for the mills of the angels rested to sanctify the Lord and the double portion of the day remained pure. Nonetheless, Abiram and Dathan and others with them, went out, despite the Sabbath, desiring to gather a larger provision. When they realized that no manna had fallen that day they began to fear that it would fall no more.

But Moses said to them, "O you sinners! God commands that you rest and you do not obey him. How, then, will you observe his law? Keep the Sabbath and God will give you the Promised Land and the world to come."

Then they listened to him, but if all the children of Israel had, from the first moment, respected the Sabbath, no nation on earth would have vanquished Israel.

Thus, our doctors comment, for 40 years the Lord did for the children of Israel in the desert what Abraham at Mamre had done for the three angels of the Lord. Abraham had offered the angels water—God opened for the Israelites Miriam's well. Abraham had offered the angels bread—God opened for his children his reservoirs of manna. Abraham had offered to the angels the shade of his trees—God put forth over the children of Israel the shadow of his splendor. Abraham had offered to lead the angels back—God led the children of Israel by his miraculous pillar.

For, our sages add, the Lord is in no way like an earthly king who says to his servant, "Serve me, so I may eat; serve me, so I may drink; dress me; bear before me a torch." It was God, the Master, who, when he chose Israel for his servant, gave him meat and drink and dressed him in his splendor and illumined him with his light.

But Israel became accustomed to all these favors. What at first had seemed incredible now seemed but natural and, forgetting God who had bestowed upon them his miracles, they were, say our rabbis, like the child perched on his father's shoulder to whom his father gives all sorts of playthings, but who asks each newcomer, "Where is my father?" Then what does the father do? Annoyed, he throws the child down whereupon the dog runs up and the child is bitten.

The dog who bit Israel was Amalek.

The son of Eliphaz, the eldest son of Jacob's enemy brother Esau, had inherited his ancestor's hatred and sought the extermination of Israel to fulfill the charge his ancestors had levied on his heirs. In his hatred he sent envoys to all the nations of the earth saying, "Do not scorn these fugitives who have come out from Egypt to free themselves from slavery. Attack them in the desert, while they are still destitute. Do not wait until they are strengthened and, swollen with vanity by the capture of some town or territory, decide themselves to declare war upon you."

But remembering God's wonders and fearing the fate of the Egyptians, these nations dared not join him. Only Amalek, Israel's brother, alone with his men attacked them from the land of Seir. Without provocation he and his troops rose up against Israel.

At first, camped in front of the children of Israel, he tried to draw them out with soft words. "Are we not brothers?" he said. "Come, let us converse together; accept the gifts that I give you."

Those whom he was able to seduce he slaughtered. Mutilating their bodies, he hurled their dismembered limbs that bore upon them the seal of the covenant towards heaven crying, "Behold your covenant with the Eternal."

Whom could Moses choose from among the descendants of Jacob to fight against this evil brother? For had not Reuben, Simeon and Levi, Judah, Naphtali, Dan and Gad, Asher, Issachar and Zebulun all sold their brother Joseph? For that reason Moses chose Joshua, the son of Nun, descended from Joseph, who when he was sold by his brothers pardoned them, for only the prince in whose veins flowed truly brotherly blood was pure enough to chastise the sin against brotherhood.

So Moses told Joshua all that he must do. Then he said to the Israelites, "You only have to fight against men but God is with you. He who opened for you a path through the waters and a path through thirst and hunger will not abandon you now."

Moses filled them with such brave courage that they themselves clamored for battle.

Then he went up to the top of the hill with Aaron his brother and Hur the husband of Miriam his sister where he beseeched the Lord, "King of the World," he cried, "it is by my hands but by your power that you have delivered your people. It was by my hand but by your power that you divided the waters and vanquished our hunger and thirst. May it be your power today that

shall bring victory, for my hand, without your power, is nothing."
And from the top of the hill he looked upon the mêlée.

It came to pass that when Moses held up his hands, Israel
prevailed but when he let fall his hands Amalek prevailed. But
Moses could not hold up his hands all the time for sometimes
doubt weakened him. Seeing this, Hur and Aaron held up his two
hands until the going down of the sun and the defeat of Amalek.

Why, our rabbis inquire, was this miracle performed? Was it
Moses' raised hands that brought victory? In no wise, but he
endeavored with prayer while the Israelites fought with arms and
his prayer strengthened their arms.

The slaughter of the Amalekites was so great that their dead
could not be numbered while Israel suffered no loss. No other
victory had such consequences, for besides the terror with which
it filled the nations, it put courage into the hearts of the children
of Israel. No longer, as in the days of the divided waters, or of the
welling rock, or of the sustaining manna, was it God alone or God
with his Prophet who had decided their fate. They themselves by
fighting had made proof of their faith and had seen that with faith
nothing is impossible. Thus Moses, wishing to perpetuate the glory
of this miracle, built an altar of stone which God called "My
Miracle" for the greatest of God's miracles is Israel's faith.

When Jethro, with Zipporah his daughter, Moses' wife, and the
two sons she had borne him, heard of these marvels, he came from
Midian into the wilderness of Sinai to seek the Prophet in the
place where the Lord had appeared to him in the burning bush.
When he neared the camp, Jethro sent a message to the Prophet
of the Israelites, saying, "When I, with Balaam and Job, counseled
Pharaoh in Egypt in the days before you were born, I had already
felt that the God of Israel is a great God. Since then I have visited
all the idols of all the temples of the earth and seen that every idol
is vanity. Before your coming to Midian I had seen that the idol

of Midian, that I served, was also vanity. Now I know that only the God of Israel is God, maker of heaven and earth. Receive me, then, among his people. If you will not do it for me, do it for Zipporah, your wife, whom I bring back to you. If you will not do it for her, do it for your sons whom I bring back to you."

Moses pondered this in his heart, "Should I receive them? While the children of Israel baked bricks and covered over with lime their sacrificed children under the whip of slavery, *they* were at ease in Midian. While the children of Israel groaned with hunger and thirsted in the wilderness, they in Midian were rich and carefree. Now the Lord is about to give the children of Israel his law, the reward of their sufferings, and shall they who have suffered nothing for his law also have part in it?"

But God said to Moses, "Am I then only the God of those who are near me? Every heart that turns toward me is with me."

At once Moses rose up and, followed by the 70 elders, by Aaron and by Aaron's four sons, he went toward the gates of the camp to meet Jethro. When Jethro the proselyte entered into the camp, behold—at full noon manna began to fall for his sake only and it fell so abundantly that he could have fed all the nations of the earth with it.

Then Moses gave him the kiss of peace for the name of the Lord is Peace. And Moses made a feast for Jethro and served him at it himself.

And now, delivered from the fear of hunger and thirst, freed from the terror of warring men, exalted by the faith of the converted heathens, the children of Israel could turn their whole souls toward the promise of the law. Then it was that Job, tortured by Satan on his dunghill, unknowing in his blasphemy that his anguish was the ransom of their salvation, was suddenly restored by the Lord to his past happiness and he cried out in his joy, "Blessèd be the Lord!"

CHAPTER X

THE VOICE ON THE MOUNTAIN

When God was about to give Israel the law of Moses, which is called the Torah, all the mountains appeared before him and each cried: "King of the World, King of the World, let your splendor fall upon me, let your Torah be given from me!"

"Choose me," said Hermon. "Am I not the highest of mountains? My crown emerged from the Deluge as your law will emerge from sin."

"Choose me," said Carmel. "Am I not the loveliest of gardens? Plant upon me the garden of your law which will make the soul into a garden lovelier than Eden."

"Choose me, choose me," said Lebanon. "Am I not the most beautiful of hymns in the voice of my cedars which hymn your grandeur. Hymn upon me the hymn of your law which will make all people as a hymn toward you."

But God said to Sinai: "On you I will set my splendor; from you I will give my Torah for you are alone in the desert, as Israel my people is alone in the desert of the peoples and as I, I the Lord God, am alone in the desert of the universe."

Eternal is the Torah, say our rabbis, for it existed before the world and for it the world was; and when he created the world, the Lord consulted it.

Mighty is the Torah, say our doctors, for God decreed, "Let the heaven be my place and the earth the place of humankind."

But through the Torah, which united heaven and earth, heaven descended upon earth and earth arose into heaven.

Wise is the Torah, say our sages, for if all the water of all the seas were changed into ink and all the reeds of all the rivers into pens and if the whole extent of the whole firmament were changed into parchment, and the fingers of all the living into fingers of scribes, there would not be enough ink, nor enough parchment, nor enough pens, nor enough scribes to write the whole wisdom of the Torah.

Great is the Torah—greater than truth, for it contains truth; greater than justice, for it contains justice; greater than love and greater than mercy, for the Torah contains mercy and the Torah contains love.

But, our rabbis ask, if God possessed such a treasure and if he wished to give it to mortals, why did he not give it to the first person on the first day? The first humans received from the Lord a single commandment, "You shall not eat of the fruit of this tree." Yet Adam ate of the fruit. How then could he have received the 613 commandments of the Torah?

Why did God not give it to the generation of Noah? Noah received from the eternal seven commandments and his descendants built Babel. How then could they have received the 613 commandments of the Torah?

Why did he not give it to the generations of the Patriarchs? The Patriarchs received from the eternal nine commandments and their descendants merited the slavery of Egypt. How then could they have received the 613 commandments of the Torah?

The generation of Moses was purified by the sufferings of bondage, by hunger and thirst and by the witness of miracles. Now peace reigned among the children of Israel and living in peace they could receive the Torah of Moses which is the Peace of the Lord. Each day after the departure from Egypt, the Prophet asked the Lord, "When will you give us the Torah?" But still the Lord delayed.

God waited until the month of Sivan, which is the third among the months. Like a king of flesh and blood who before he leads his betrothed beneath the nuptial canopy first loads her with gifts, he first wanted to give the children of Israel the well and the manna before marrying, through the Torah, the community of Israel.

He waited until the month of Sivan, which is the third among the months, because the number three rejoices the Lord. It was the third son of Adam, Seth, who was the ancestor of humankind. It was the third son of Noah, Shem, who was the ancestor of Israel. It was the three Patriarchs—Abraham, Isaac and Jacob—who by their virtue merited the glory of the chosen people. It was in the third tribe, that of Levi, that Moses was born, who was the third child of his mother. For three months his existence was concealed before he was put into the cradle which saved him upon the river and for three months the Lord concealed upon the mountain the Torah which should save humankind.

When the month of Sivan had come, God said to Moses, "The soul of my Torah is without blemish. Is the body of my people without blemish? There are among them the deaf and the mute, the blind and the lame. Shall I give my Torah to those who cannot see it nor hear it, who can neither sing nor dance for it?"

What, then, did God do? He restored their voices to the mute and their hearing to the deaf; he restored their eyes to the blind and to the lame their legs. Thus it shall be in the world to come when the deaf shall hear, when the blind shall see, when the lame and the mute shall dance and sing before the Lord.

Now, as sound in flesh as in spirit, they could receive the Torah. But would they desire to welcome it? The Torah is a crown, but a crown is a burden; the Torah is a necklace, but a necklace is a chain. God had offered it to all the peoples of the earth, so that none could say, "If we had known it, we would have practiced it," and he gave it, not in a land shut in by frontiers, but in the midst of the wilderness, so that any who wanted it might take it, as it is written, *The Lord came from Sinai and rose up from Seir unto them; he shined forth from Mount Paran; from his right hand went a fiery law for them.*

He went first to the children of Esau and asked them, "Do you desire my Torah?"

They replied, "What does it command?"

"You shall not kill."

"Then we would have to renounce the blessing of Esau, our father, who blessed us saying, 'You shall live by the sword.' We do not want your Torah."

He went next to the children of Ammon and Moab and asked them, "Do you desire my Torah?"

They replied, "What does it command?"

"You shall not commit fornication."

"We were born from fornication," they replied. "We do not want your Torah."

Then he went to the children of Ishmael and asked them, "Do you desire my Torah?"

They replied, "What does it command?"

"You shall not steal."

"How then should we find meat and drink?" they replied. "We do not want your Torah."

And then he went to all the other people, who all replied to him, "We have our law; give your Torah to Israel, for Israel is free and has no law."

Then the Lord called Moses to the mountain and Moses went up toward God and God commanded him, "Ask the children of Israel if they desire my Torah."

Moses addressed himself first of all to the women. Why the women? Because, Rabbi Tahlipha says, the Prophet thought in his heart, "If God had instructed Eve, would Adam have sinned?" For he knew that everything depends on woman, who at her pleasure brings salvation or ruin upon the world.

So having assured himself of the women's acquiescence, he assembled the whole people, men and women, the old and the young and he said, "Hard is the beginning of all things and harder than all is the beginning of obedience, but you have begun to obey and he who at first obeys in pain soon obeys in joy, and to obey God is the greatest of joys. Your eyes have seen what miracles he did for you, delivering you from Egypt, from thirst and from hunger. And yet you had not then received his Torah. What miracles will he not do when you have received it, listened to it, followed it? Then he will bear you on the wings of the eagle and to the end of time he will watch over you like the swallow over her young. But when the Torah belongs to you, you will belong to the Torah. All the blessings which are in it will be yours, if you follow it. If you abandon it, all the curses that are in it will fall upon you. Now, answer God. Do you desire his Torah?"

And the children of Israel said, "We desire it. What it commands, that will we do."

"But," Moses then asked them, "what will be the guarantee of your promise before the Lord?"

"Let the Elders be our guarantors," they said.

"Your Elders will die, so how can they be your guarantors?"

"Let our Patriarchs be our guarantors."

"Your Patriarchs are dead; how can they be your guarantors?"

"Let our prophets be our guarantors."

"Your prophets are unborn; how can they be your guarantors?"

Then the women of Israel said to the Prophet, "Let our children be their guarantors; God will teach you the Torah, you will teach it to the parents, they will teach it to the children and the

children to their children and the children of their children to
their children's children."

And Moses asked the children, "Will you be the guarantors of
your parents before the Lord?"

They answered, "We will."

Then all the children of Israel cried, "Our children will be our
guarantors; everything the Lord commands, we will hear and do,
but let God himself show us his face. Let him speak to us with his
own voice."

When Moses brought back to the Lord on the mountain the
Israelites' answer, God said to him, "For two days let them sanctify themselves and keep themselves from their wives; on the third
day they shall see me and shall hear me. Let none of them go up
into the mountain, for they would die, and you yourself, my son,
go down."

Why, our rabbis ask, did Moses have to go down and stay
away, in the midst of the Israelites, when God spoke to them? Was
not God always near Moses and was not Moses accustomed to
hearing the Lord? But if, when God spoke, Moses had stayed on
the mountain, near God, Abiram and Dathan would have said to
the Israelites, "It is not God, it is Moses who is speaking," and the
Israelites would have doubted whether it was God.

Now the summer night was so short and the morning sleep so
sweet that on the third morning, which was the sixth of the
month of Sivan, when God descended upon Sinai before Israel, all
the children of Israel were still asleep. Moses, who alone was
awake, went through the whole camp waking each one. "Rise up,"
he said. "O Israel, shake off your slumber; your spouse awaits his
betrothed beneath the nuptial canopy."

Going first, followed by Aaron and his sons and by all the
men, all the women and all the children, Moses led the entire
congregation to the foot of the mount over which, as a nuptial

canopy, there hung a cloud.

Then the majesty of the spouse was attested to by the mingled roaring of thunder and the blaring of trumpets upon Sinai. The invisible presence, with lightnings shattering through wind and tempest, hail and fire, filled with awful tumult and quaking the upper and the nether deeps.

All the kings of the world in anguished terror sought out Balaam, the prophet of the nations and, trembling, asked him, "Is it the Flood beginning anew?"

"Fools! Do you not know that the God of Israel gave his promise to Noah that he would never again loose upon the earth the waters of the Flood?"

"If it is not a flood of waters, is it a flood of fire?"

"It is a flood neither of waters nor of flames; it is the God of Israel who is giving to his people his Torah."

The earth also shuddered in fear, "Is it the Judgment Day?" she cried. "Shall I have to give up the dead I have eaten and the blood I have drunk?"

Moses answered, "It is not the world ending, but the world beginning."

The heavens shook and wept, "Our king is abandoning us; he is leaving his kingdom."

"No," answered the prophet, "God is not abandoning the kingdom of the skies. He is extending his frontiers to the hearts of people."

And the Lord himself was sorrowful. "Why are you sorrowful," asked Moses, "when you are giving them your law?"

"You see that I am giving it to them," the Lord answered, "but I see what they will do with it."

Suddenly the cloud opened, Sinai tore out its roots from the wilderness and, hurtling into the firmament, its broad summit came to rest beneath the flaming feet and flaming wings of the Four Beasts: the Four Beasts with the heads of a human, of a lion, of an eagle and of a bull, harnessed to the many-eyed wheels that revolve like suns beneath the Chariot whose splendor bore the Throne, whose splendor bore the splendor of the Lord. And all around 120 hosts of angels, each one of whom carried a belt of glory and a crown of glory for each one of the children of Israel, cried out unceasingly, "Holy, Holy, Holy is the Lord of Sabaoth. The whole world is full of his glory."

Suddenly, as God was about to speak, there was silence in all the universe. Not an ox lowed in all the earth, not a bird twittered in all the skies. The waters ceased their murmur, the flames their crackling, the thunder was muted, every echo was muted, the wings of the Cherubim ceased to beat and the mouths of the Seraphim to sing, in order, says Rabbi Abbahu, that in the silence of all things, all things might know that outside God there is nothing.

Then the Lord spoke, saying, I AM.

As these words resounded, filling all space with their vastness, all the children of Israel, except Moses, fled and their souls fled from their bodies. The Torah returned towards God, asking, "King of the World, are you sending me to the living or to the dead?"

"To the living."

"But all are dead."

"For you, let them be resurrected." And God rained upon them the dew that revives the dead. But since, when they were resurrected, they could sustain neither the weight of his Word nor the sight of his splendor, God sent two angels to each of the children of Israel, one to put over their hearts belts of glory so their souls should not depart from them and the other to place on their heads crowns of glory so their eyes should not die. And thus they could at once both hear and see the Word of splendor for, our rabbis say, on that day they saw what is heard and heard what is seen.

And the Word of splendor said, "Behold, I am the One God and I show myself to you in my only splendor. If one day you are tempted and one says to you, 'Come, let us serve other gods,' you shall answer him, 'Can one serve another god who has seen, face to face, the One God in his splendor?' Behold, I am the God of every people, yet with Israel alone I make a covenant that through Israel I may be joined to all peoples. Behold, I am God, merciful and everlasting, just and long-suffering, abounding in grace and in truth, if you obey me, my gifts shall prove my tenderness; if you disobey, my chastising shall prove my love. Do not take my name in vain, for upon my name the world is established and those who profane my name destroy the world.

"Remember the Sabbath to keep it holy, for the Sabbath is the beginning, in this world, of the world to come. Honor your father and your mother, for by honoring the ones who created you, you will honor your Creator. You shall not kill, for murder compels the God of mercy to vengeance. You shall not commit adultery. You shall not steal. You shall not bear false witness. You shall not covet...."

Each of these words, after touching the ear of each of the children of Israel, rested upon their mouths and kissed their mouths, as it is written, *Let him kiss me with the kisses of his mouth.*

And not only Israel heard these words, but the 70 nations of the earth heard them also, for the Lord uttered them in 70 languages simultaneously. And not only the living heard them, but also all no longer alive and all those yet unborn for, according to the teaching of Rabbi Isaac, all the souls of all the ages were present at Sinai—all the Prophets, all the sages heard there and in that hour all the voices and saw there and in that hour all the visions, which throughout all the ages they had revealed and were to reveal to all humankind. And all heard the same voice and saw the same

vision, but, according as each was or would be different, the voice
and the vision were different for each.

When the Lord had spoken his first Ten Commandments to
the children of Israel and they had accepted them, all evil left
them. Then God asked them, "Israel, do you wish for my whole
Torah with its 365 prohibitions, numerous as the days of a person's year, and its 247 injunctions, numerous as the organs of a
person's body?"

All answered, "Yes, yes."

But in spite of the angels who supported them and the crowns
and belts of glory that bound them, they cried to Moses, "We
demanded to see him and hear him, we can bear it no longer. We
are too fragile for his voice, too delicate for his face. Let him show
himself to you, let him speak to you. You will show us what he
shall show you; what he shall tell you, you will tell us."

And then evil re-entered them, but if they had been able to
look upon the Lord to the end and to the end had heard him, they
never would have sinned again.

Moses said to them, "Go down from the mount. I will go up
alone to God."

CHAPTER XI

THE SCHOOL ON HIGH

It is written, *Moses went into the midst of the cloud.* As to this, our sages have told us that in the hour when Moses went up into the mountain, a cloud came to rest in front of him. He did not know whether he should step into it or cling to it with his hands. But the cloud opened; the Prophet entered in and it bore him to the heavens.

First he passed the first heaven where two angels watch each gate—the gates of prayer and of supplication, of joy and of sorrow, of abundance and of famine, of war and of peace, of conception and of birth, of health and of disease, of life and of death.

In the second heaven he saw the angel Nuriel, with his 50 hosts of angels who rule the clouds and the waves, the dew and the tempest, and in the third heaven, the palace with pillars of red fire, beams of green fire, ceiling of blue fire and walls of fiery white where dwell the angels who rule the sun and the moon and all the lesser lights.

At the entrance to the fourth heaven the angel Kemuel, with his 12,000 destroying angels, stopped him, crying, "Man born of woman and of sin, what do you come to seek among the holy ones of the Most High?"

"I am the son of Amram," Moses answered, "and I come to receive the Torah from the Lord."

As Kemuel was about to seize him with his flaming hand, Moses, striking him, flung him from the world.

Then, pursuing his way, the Prophet climbed 60 times 10,000 parasangs to the fifth heaven, where dwells Hadarniel, whose every word darts forth 70,000 lightnings. "Man born of woman and of sin, what do you come to seek among the holy ones of the Most High?" cried the Angel.

When Moses heard his voice, his eyes melted to tears and his soul to terror and he would have hurled himself from the cloud-top into the abyss. But the Lord was moved with compassion and a daughter of the Voice was heard in sternness, "From the first hours of the world, you angels whom I have created, you have been the fomenters of quarrelling. When I wanted to create Adam, you came to accuse him before me, saying, 'What, then, is man that you should consider him?' and I had to burn you in hosts in order to fulfil the work of my love. Know, then, that if I had not created man, the world would have been chaos and if I do not give him my Torah, to chaos the world will return."

At these words Hadarniel was calmed and said, "You know, Lord, I was ignorant of your wish. If it is by your wish that he come, I will receive him as a disciple receives the master."

And, as a disciple accompanies the master, so did he lead Moses by a path that would have taken a mortal 500 years to climb to the sixth heaven, where he left him, saying, "This far it is permitted me to climb, higher I cannot. Sandalfon's fire would devour me."

Sandalfon weaves crowns for the Holy One, blessèd be he, and places them on his head. But how can an angel, our sages ask, crown the Holiest in the Highest? He cannot. When Sandalfon has woven a crown, he implores the crown, which of itself rises and crowns the head of the Holy One. Then all the armies of the heights tremble together with the wheels of the heavenly chariot and his heavenly footstool and the heavenly beasts of his heavenly team, with all the angels of the crown and the crown itself, cry out, "Blessed is the glory of the Lord from his place."

When Moses saw Sandalfon, his eyes melted to tears and his soul to terror and he would have thrown himself from the cloud-top into the abyss. But look how cherished was the Prophet to the Holy One, blessèd be he! In that hour the Holy One, blessèd be he, himself descended from his throne and placed between his Prophet and his angel, his splendor, so that the Prophet might pass. And when he had passed before Rigjion, who examines the secrets of the eternal and before Gelizur, who proclaims his decrees, Moses entered the school of the Most High. There in semicircles the angels are ranged and the angel Zagzagel teaches them from the Torah.

When Moses had entered, a clamor arose from all the ranged angels, "Zagzagel, Zagzagel, will you teach the Torah of the Lord to this human? Will he not say to humankind, 'It is *my* Torah'?"

Then the Torah itself rose up. On its right was the archangel Michael, on its left the archangel Gabriel. Uriel was before and Raphael behind and they bore four standards on which blazed the east and the west, the north and the south. And the Torah said, "King of the World, has not this man obeyed me even before knowing me? Has he not proclaimed your name, kept the Sabbath, honored his father and his mother? Has he not kept his mouth from lies and blasphemy, his hand from theft and from murder, his flesh from sin and his soul from envy? What does it matter then, Lord, if one day he says your Torah is *his* Torah? He who obeys your Torah, is he not as if he had created it?"

And the Holy One, blessèd be he, replied, "Moses, come sit above the angels. I, myself, will teach you my Torah."

Now the Torah contains all things and Moses first saw in it the six things which, with it, were created before the Creation—these are: penitence, Gehenna, the Garden of Eden, the sanctuary, the throne and the glory of the Messiah.

In the river of Purgatory, Adam was immersed, doing penance. The wicked who passed by, being led to Gehenna, said to him,

"Why did you not come with us to atone for our sins? Are you not the author of all our sinning?"

He answered the wicked, "I sinned but once; your sins are your own."

The righteous who passed by, going toward the Garden of Eden, said to him, "You have but one sin, ours are countless. Why does yours remain, if ours are effaced?"

Adam answered them, "My one sin contained all yours; until the death of sin I must do penance."

When Moses entered Gehenna, the fires of Gehenna withdrew from before him 5,000 parasangs and Nasargiel, the angel of Gehenna, asked the Prophet, "Who are you?"

"I am the son of Amram."

"Your place is not here; it is in the Garden of Eden."

"I am come to see, in Gehenna, the justice of God."

Then Nasargiel showed him the tortures of the damned and the place called Alukah and the place called Tit ha-Yawen and the place called Abaddon, where all the damned cry out to death, "Death, death, give us death!"

Then Moses said to God, "King of the World, save me, save Israel from Gehenna."

But God answered him, "The Lord shows no favor, neither for you nor for Israel. Whoever does evil falls into Gehenna; whoever does good ascends into the Garden of Eden."

When Moses entered the Garden of Eden, the light of the Garden advanced before him 5,000 parasangs and Shamshiel, the angel of the Garden of Eden, asked him, "Who are you?"

"I am the son of Amram."

"Your place is not here; it is on earth."

"I have come to witness in the Garden of Eden the justice of God."

Then Shamshiel showed him the 70,000 sweet-smelling trees of the Garden of Eden, the least of which is more delightful than all the trees of earth and bears 5,000 different fruits, not one of whose savors is like the savors of earth. He showed him the righteous clothed in glory and holding in their hands branches of myrrh, seated beneath canopies embroidered with golden vines, before tables of pearl, upon seats of sapphire from which flow four rivers—one of milk, one of honey, one of wine and one of balm. He also showed him the highest of these seats which are those of Abraham, of Isaac and of Jacob. When the Patriarchs saw Moses they blessed him, saying, "Blessèd be he who fulfills our promises."

And the Prophet replied, "Who blesses in the name of the Lord, blessèd be he."

When Moses entered the sanctuary on high, Metatron, the angel of the sanctuary, said to him, "Behold and you will make a sanctuary on earth."

The veils of the sanctuary—white, violet, purple and crimson—were made from the angels' wings. The torch of the sanctuary was of stars and the table of endless fields. The basin contained seas and upon the altar of sacrifice there burned prayers and upon the altar of incense souls rose in exhalation.

When Moses entered before the Throne of splendor he saw around the Throne the Seraphim who have each six wings as wide and as long as the space between earth and heaven. Two of these wings sway, hymning the Lord; two are lowered to hide from his sight the sins of humankind and the two highest are raised to hide from the Seraphim the blaze of his splendor. When Moses appeared they stopped swaying their wings, for his presence was a hymn; they ceased from lowering their wings, for his presence hid sin; but they still veiled their faces before the blaze of the splendor which the Prophet gazed upon face to face.

When Moses appeared before the Messiah, the head of the Messiah was adorned with seven diadems of gold. And the Holy One, blessèd be he, showing Moses to him, said, "This is he who is beginning your work. Will you wish to complete it? He has delivered Israel from the slavery of Egypt; you will deliver human-kind from the bondage of sin. He has given Israel water and manna; you will give humankind peace and justice. he, teaching the precepts of the Torah, will lead Israel to the Land of Promise; you, fulfilling the promises of the Torah, will make a Land of Promise of all the earth. But the sinners, by their sins, will put an iron yoke upon you. They will stifle your breath. Your tongue will cleave to the roof of your mouth. The whole anguish of all the earth and of all the ages will be your anguish. Is your will for these things?"

And the Messiah replied, "In the joy of my heart will I accept all suffering, provided that none in Israel shall be lost and that none outside Israel shall be lost and that all shall be helped by my help—not only those who will be living in my days, but those also who will be hidden in the earth; not only those who will have died in my days, but those also who will have died from the first day to my day; not only those who have died after having lived, but those also who are born dead and those also whom you have thought of creating, but have not created, O Lord. If all the sons of Adam and Adam himself are saved by my agony, I will accept all agony. Thus learn the Torah, O Moses, you will teach it; I shall fulfil it."

Then, in order to learn the Torah, Moses remained 40 days and 40 nights without eating or drinking. Is it possible, Rabbi Meir demands, for a human to go 40 nights and 40 days without food or drink? Moses, he answers, observed like the angels the saying, *When you are in a city, do as the inhabitants thereof.* Just as when the angels came down, for Abraham's sake, upon the earth where people eat and drink, so they ate and they drank. When Moses went up for the Lord's sake into heaven where the angels neither eat nor drink, he neither ate nor drank.

And, Rabbi Eleazar bar Ahin asks, how could Moses know, so close and in the presence of God, whether it was night or day? For are not the shadows, near God, brightness? But when Moses saw the sun bow down before the Holy One, blessèd be he, he knew that on earth it was night. When he saw the moon and the stars bow down before the Holy One, blessèd be he, he knew that on earth it was day.

For 40 days and 40 nights Moses studied the Torah, thereby teaching the children of Israel that they must study the Torah by night and day for the Torah contains precepts for all things—for feasting and for fasting, for clothing and for shelter, for sowing and for harvest, for humans and for beast, for rich and for poor, for war and for peace, for sorrow and for joy, for prayer and for offerings, for sacrifice and for repentance, for punishment and for mercy, for justice and for love.

For 40 days and 40 nights Moses studied the Torah. To merit a king's crown only three virtues are needed; a pontiff's crown requires only 24, but the crown of the Torah requires more than 40. Look, says Rabbi Hija bar Abba, how much greater is the Torah than the world, to give the world to the world, God needed only seven days; he needed a full 40 to give to it the Torah.

Thus for 40 days and 40 nights Moses studied the Torah, but what he learned each day, he forgot each night and what he learned each night, he forgot each day. And he said to the Lord, "It is in vain you teach, in vain I learn, for the Torah is the Torah and Moses is but Moses."

What did God do? He took two tables of sapphire which he had created on the eve of the first Sabbath, at the last moment of Creation, and with his own hand he inscribed on them for Moses the Torah. These two tables were only six feet wide and six feet long, yet he was able to write on them the Ten Commandments and, between the lines of the Ten Commandments, the 247 precepts and the 365 prohibitions of the Torah. The tables were such that the writing could be read above the stone and beneath the stone and through the stone and, although this stone was the hardest of stones, it rolled up like parchment and had no weight.

While God wrote upon the sapphire, Moses saw strokes and signs traced like crowns linked to the letters of the Torah. He asked the Holy One, blessèd be he, "King of the World, what are these signs? What are these strokes? Would not the letters be sufficient without their crowns?"

God answered him, "After generations and generations a man shall arise, Akiba his name, and upon each of these strokes and these signs he will heap up new thoughts."

"King of the World," said Moses, "permit me to see him."

"Return and go."

Moses turned, went and sat down in the eighth row in Akiba's school and he heard the doctor teaching the Torah to his disciples, but he could not understand this Torah, for the Torah Akiba taught was full of new thoughts which God had not taught to Moses in his Torah.

Now Akiba's disciples asked their master, "Rabbi, from where have you received this Torah?"

The rabbi replied to his disciples, "From the Torah given by God to Moses upon Sinai."

Then the Prophet questioned the Lord saying, "How is this thing possible? I do not recognize the Torah you gave me. Is this new Torah your Torah?"

God answered him, "There are 50 gateways of understanding. I have opened for you 49, but the last is closed, for no human, even be he Moses, my son, can know everything. The Torah, you understand, has a thousand senses which you understand not and which others, in the course of the ages, will come to know, for in each century it will speak the language of that century, but what each century will find is already there and each new Torah will still be my Torah."

"But why will Akiba come so late in the centuries?" Moses asked again. "And why, Lord, choose a Moses when you have an Akiba?"

"Be silent, for such is my decree: Moses is proper to the days of Moses, Akiba to the days of Akiba."

"Then, Lord, show me his reward."

"Turn, go and look!"

Moses turned, went and looked and he saw Akiba torn apart by iron combs. "King of the World," he cried, "is this his wage?"

"Be silent, for such is my decree. The wicked receive upon earth the reward for their few good deeds and in Gehenna the punishment for all their wickedness. The good receive upon earth the punishment for their few evil deeds and in the Garden of Eden the reward for all their good ones."

And now the hour had come when the Lord would confide into the hands of the Prophet the tables of sapphire. Then Samael, the angel of death, rose up from the abyss. He was so huge that it would take seven times 500 years to go from his feet to his head. From head to foot he was covered with eyes that watched fixedly.

Moses implored the Lord, saying, "Lord God and God of my ancestors, let me never fall into his hands."

"Be silent," God answered him, "for such is my decree. All people must die. But if the children of Israel observe my Torah, Israel shall never die. For I, the eternal, myself obey this Torah that today I give to you. By this same law that divides the Sabbath from the other days I have divided night from day and I leave them divided. By this same law that divides Israel from the other peoples, I have divided the land from the sea and I leave them divided. By this same law that divides good from evil, I have divided the world from chaos and I leave them divided.

"Behold I am not like an earthly monarch who gives a gift, but withholds himself. I give you my Torah and with my Torah I give myself to you. I am in no way like an earthly monarch who commands servants but never obeys them, for if you command me, you my Prophet, in the name of my law, I, your Lord, in the name of my law, will obey you.

"Now remember that in my Torah justice and mercy are commingled, for if it were all mercy, how would sin not destroy the world? And if it were all justice, how would justice not destroy the sinner? Thus, since it is permitted you to see me face to face, when my face is justice let yours be mercy."

As Moses received into his hands the tables of sapphire, the splendor of the Torah lit his face and this splendor never left him after. He blessed the Torah, saying, "Praise be to you, O Lord our God, who chooses your law and chooses your people and who blesses your people when it chooses your law."

But other angels had risen up around Samael—Af, the angel of wrath, Hemah, Dumah and Mavet, Raguel, Sariel and Jerahmiel and with them the Arelim, the Malakim, the Hashmallim, the Shinannim, the Tarshishim and the Ofanim, crying, "King of the World, King of the World, will you then confide to dust and nothingness the Torah that is your wisdom, your treasure, your vastness?"

"Answer them," said the Lord to the Prophet.

"They will burn me with their breath."

"Take hold of my throne of glory and answer them."

Then Moses said to them, "What is there in this Torah that God desires to give me? *I am the Lord your God, which brought you out of the land of Egypt, out of the house of bondage.* Did you go into Egypt, angels of heaven, did you serve Pharaoh? *You shall have no other gods before me.* Did you live among idolaters; did you have to break your idols? *Remember the Sabbath day, to keep it holy.* What is your work, that from it you must rest? *Honor your father and your mother.* Where are your fathers, where your mothers, to be honored? *You shall not kill, you shall not steal, you shall not commit adultery.* Do you then know murder, envy, lust? The Torah of heaven is made for earth, let it descend to earth."

But all the angels crushed around Moses in a flaming multitude, wanting to destroy him. Then God threw over the Prophet's shoulders the mantle of his invisible glory and said to him, "Go down."

So Moses went down, bearing in his arms the Tables of the Torah and on his face its splendor.

In this very hour, according to Rabbi Johanan ben Levi, Satan appeared before the Lord and asked him, "King of the World, where is the Torah?"

"I have given it to the earth."

Satan went to the earth and asked her, "Where is the Torah?"

The earth answered, "God knows its way, he alone knows its place."

He went to the sea, which cried, "It is not with me," to the abyss, which cried, "Neither with me," to pestilence and death, who cried, "We have heard tell of it, but where it is we know not." Satan returned to God, saying, "King of the World, I have sought the Torah through all the earth and have found it not."

"Go to the son of Amram."

And Satan went to Moses who was going down the mountain and asked him, "Where is the Torah that the Lord has given you?"

Moses, who had hidden the Torah beneath the mantle of invisible glory, answered him, "Who am I, that the Lord should have given me the Torah?"

Then God chided the Prophet, "What, my son, you have lied?"

But Moses answered before the face of the Lord, "King of the World, you had a hidden treasure, which was your joy to you each day—and *I* would have boasted its possession?"

And God said to his servant, "Since you perceive yourself as small before the Torah, behold, it shall be called by your name." Thus it is written, *Remember the Torah of Moses, my servant.*

CHAPTER XII

THE GOLDEN CALF

For 40 days Joshua, son of Nun, had awaited Moses upon the slopes of the mount. When the Prophet rejoined him, suddenly they both heard a commotion rising up to them.

"I hear a noise of war," said Joshua.

"Man of war," replied Moses, "it is not the voice of those who shout for victory, neither is it the voice of those crying in defeat, but rather those are voices of people crying out to an idol."

Then Joshua, with his younger stride outstripping the Prophet, ran to the camp of the Israelites.

As Moses went, the word of the Lord thundered through space, "Go down, Moses. Your people have denied me."

"Why do you call them *my* people?" asked the Prophet. "Were they not *your* people when you commanded me, 'Go bring up out of Egypt my people Israel'? I said to you then, 'They are stained with sin.' And you answered me, 'I will take away their sin.' And now, because your wrath is kindled against *your* children, you call them *my* children."

"They are my children when they obey; when they do not obey they are no longer mine."

"Where have you brought them up, that they should remain pure? You made them grow up in the land of graven images, and you would have them worship you?"

"But have I not saved them out of Egypt? Did I not divide the waters to set them free?"

"How long ago? Yesterday they were slaves and today you expect them to be adults?"

To what may we liken the matter? asks Rab Huna. To that sage who opened a perfume shop for his son in the street of harlots. One evening having caught him with a courtesan he was going to thrash him, but a friend caught his arm, saying, "None of the trades of the city and none of the streets of the city were good enough for your son, so you set him up as a perfumer in the street of harlots and you are surprised that he frequents courtesans?" In the same way Moses said to God, "None of the honors on earth and none of the lands of earth were good enough for Israel, so you made them slaves in the land of idolaters and you think they will not be idolaters?"

To what may we liken the matter? asks Rabbi Simeon ben Jehozadok. To that king who bought a field and told his gardener to plant a vine in it. The gardener dug the field and planted the vine, which grew and yielded wine, but the wine was sour.

"What is the good of this vine? Pull it up," the king ordered.

"Why," asked the gardener, "because its wine is not sweet? It is still too young. Let me tend it and its wine will be sweet."

In the same way Moses said to the Lord, "Israel has scarcely left their slavery and idolatry. Their souls are still wild. Let me teach them and they will soften. Look at your people Israel, O Lord. Are they not already less distant from your splendor? In Egypt when I spoke unto them your name, did they not believe me?"

"But since, they have stoned you."

"When they passed dryshod through the sea, did they not sing unto you a song?"

"But since, they have blasphemed me."

"Were they not, upon Sinai, the one people to accept your Torah—which all other peoples had refused?"

"But since, they have transgressed. Each time I have pardoned them. I am weary of pardon. I have said, *The idolater shall die.* Upon my life, they shall, surely."

When Moses entered the camp of the children of Israel he saw the idol standing there. It was a calf of gold. Before the golden calf was a golden altar and, beside the altar, Aaron. The Israelites were dancing and singing, "This is our god, the god of Egypt, that shall lead us back into Egypt." Dancing and singing, they were offering upon the altar to this god the manna of God.

The Prophet took up a hammer and with his mighty arms smashed the idol and made of it dust of gold upon the dust of sand. Then lifting up the hammer against Aaron his brother he cried, "How have you permitted this thing?"

"You did not return, Moses, my brother," Aaron answered him, "and Satan went all about the Israelites, saying, 'He will not return.' One day they sought out Eleazar and Ithamar, my sons, and Phinehas and Caleb, crying, 'Moses will not return; we no longer have a god; make us a god.' My sons would not, nor Caleb nor Phinehas. Then Satan made your likeness float between earth and heaven in the likeness of a shroud and they went to seek the Elders crying, 'Moses is dead; we no longer have a god; make us a god.' As the Elders would not, they said, 'Let us ourselves make us a god, a god that we can hear and see without dying, a god of Egypt, to lead us back into Egypt.' When Hur, Miriam our sister's son, sought to prevent them, they tore his body from his soul. Then I said to them, 'I myself will make you a god.' I thought in my heart, 'I will begin to make the god and, before the god is finished, Moses will return, bringing back the true God.' Thus I said to them, 'Ask your women for their jewels, out of them we will make a god.' For I thought in my heart, 'The women will not want to give them.' In truth they did refuse, for the women of Israel hold fast to their jewels and fear the eternal and because they refused, they shall be blessed among all other women. But the men brought their own nose rings, crying, 'We will kill you like we did Hur if you do not make us the god.' Was I then to let murder defile them as well as idolatry? Would the god have lived any the less had I perished? Since the sin had to be, was it not better that it should be upon me than upon them? You did not return; I finished the god."

While he spoke, the hammer, slipping from Moses' right hand, fell to the ground, but from the two tables of sapphire that the Prophet held in his left the Voice of the Lord came forth, crying, "I have said, *The idolater shall die;* upon my life, he shall, surely."

"Where have you said it," Moses asked him, "in your Torah? And to whom have you given your Torah? To them or to me?"

"Upon the mount I commanded, 'You shall have no other gods before me,' and at the foot of the mount they swore saying, 'All that God shall command we will do and hear.' "

"But did they know the punishment—death for the idolater— that your hand wrote in your Torah after this? You spared Cain because he killed not knowing the punishment for killing and yet you would punish them by a law that they did not know?"

"I will annihilate them from the face of the earth and I will make my people descend from you alone."

"Rather blot me from your Torah, King of the World, or rather let me blot from the world your Torah. I alone knew it and I alone shall have sinned if I alone shatter it."

And he brandished above his head the two tables of sapphire to cast them down to the ground. In vain did Aaron, Caleb and Joshua, Eleazar and Ithamar and the Elders, struggle to tear them from him. His giant arms outreached them. But as the Torah was leaving his opened palms, suddenly those signs engraved in the sapphire by the hand of the Lord, like a multitude of birds escaped from some vast cage and flew up to heaven. The two tables of heaven, deserted by heaven, suddenly took on the weight of earth and broke into fragments upon the earth.

To what may this be compared? asks Rabbi Samuel bar Nahman. To that envoy whom a king sent to propose marriage to a bride in his name. When the envoy came to seek her, he found she had defiled her flesh with another. What did he do? He tore up the contract of marriage, saying, "It were better for her to be judged as a maid than as a bride." In the same way Moses thought, "It were better for the congregation of Israel, since the Torah condemns them, not to be united to God by the Torah." So he shattered the Torah.

Now as soon as he had shattered it, the order of the world was shattered. The stars, the moon and the sun, which each night and each day approach the Lord to ask him to light the universe, sought him everywhere and found him no more. While they, prostrate before the harnessed beasts of the heavenly chariot, cried, "Where is God? Where is God?" the ocean, leaving its divinely ordained limits, hurled a new deluge upon the earth.

Then Moses asked the waters, "Floods from the deep, what are you doing upon the dry sand?"

"Nothing now keeps us to the deep," the waters made answer. "The world *was* only through the Torah and for the sake of sinners you have shattered the Torah."

"All those who have sinned I abandon to you," the Prophet replied, "but let Israel remain and let the world remain." And he made all the children of Israel drink of the golden dust of the idol mingled with the waters of the sea. Those who had worshiped the idol, some 3,000 sinners, perished, and the ocean withdrew.

Our doctors say that the trial of dust mingled with water was, according to the Torah of Israel, the trial of a woman taken in adultery; thus the whole congregation of Israel was subjected to it on that day of its first adultery.

But the wrath of the Lord was not appeased. He sent a pestilence to devour the camp. A voice wept from Sinai, "Weep, weep over the Torah."

Moses knelt down upon each rock of Sinai, weeping to the Lord, "Remember Marah, King of the World; there you made sweetness out of bitterness; do not now make bitterness more bitter. I have destroyed the idol and the idolaters. For 3,000 sinners must a whole people perish?"

God answered him, "Those who had not yet worshiped the golden calf were about to worship it when you arrived. From the moment you left them to go up into the mount, from the moment even when they had sworn unto me 'We will have no other gods,' in their hearts they worshiped them."

"Lord, I ask of you only what Abraham asked of you in the days of Sodom. If there be found ten righteous among them, let all be forgiven for the ten's sake."

"Where do you find them, these ten righteous?"

"Caleb, Joshua, Phinehas, Ithamar, Eleazar, Aaron and myself."

"You have only seven there."

"Is there a resurrection of the dead, King of the World?"

"What, my chid, did I not show you in the Garden of Eden that the dead rise again?"

"Then to these seven add three risen from the dead. If all these sinners have deserved exile, remember Jacob who for you went into exile to serve Laban; if they have deserved the sword, remember Isaac who for you lay under the knife of Abraham; if they deserve fire, remember Abraham who for you went into Nimrod's furnace. If you will not do this, what will these risen Patriarchs say? Did you not promise that you would lead their seed into the Promised Land? Have there been a thousand generations from theirs to mine? Did you not promise unto the thousandth generation your grace to the generations of your servants? Destroy then earth and heaven if you do not keep your word, King of the World, since it is your word that upholds heaven and earth."

At these words the heart of the Lord was softened and he said to Moses, "I will stop the pestilence and I will send an angel before Israel, to show them the way."

"Lord, every nation has an angel to lead it, but only the nation that the Lord leads dies not. Must Israel then die like another?"

"Have I not sworn, 'The idolater shall die?' Is Israel not as idolatrous as another?"

"No, no, King of the World, let Israel be your people and let their God lead them and let them go with their God wherever their God shall lead them."

The Lord answered him no more. Then Moses, feeling that the Holy One wished to forgive, took his tent and set it in the wilderness, 1,000 parasangs from the camp of the Hebrews saying, "Whom the master leaves, the servant also deserts."

Each day Aaron, his sons, the Elders and all in Levi and all in Israel went out to plead with him in his tent, "Come back to us, Moses; give us back our Torah; give back to us our God."

The Lord himself said to the Prophet, "Return to their midst. What will become of them without me if they are also without you? Did I not command you, saying, 'When my face is justice, yours shall be mercy.' "

"Why," replied Moses, "should I, who am only a human, be more merciful than you, who are God? Am I more to blame for their faults than God? When the pot breaks, do you blame the pot or the potter? The instinct of evil has perverted them. Who put it into them, they or you, Lord?"

"Moses, my son, 49 doors of understanding are opened unto you, but the 50th is closed, have I not told you? You must not yet know why God has put the instinct of evil into human beings."

"But you, did you not know their fault in advance, O Lord? When you gave me the Torah, your face was sad; already you saw them transgressing the Torah; could they then *not* transgress?"

"Humans cannot know how God can foresee everything and yet humans can be free."

"Then how shall people know if they sin or sin not? Did not your Israelites, in the days of Sinai, see, beside the likenesses of an eagle and a lion and a human, harnessed to your heavenly chariot, the likeness of a bull? Did they not think they were still worshiping you, Lord, by worshiping this likeness of a fragment of your power? Since you are in every place, since you can do all things, then share the universe with the idol so that humans may understand you. Let the idol light the sun and you the moon. Let it suffer the tempest, you the gentle winds; let it sow the rye and you the wheat; let it multiply the flesh and you the spirit."

"Moses, my son, are you blaspheming also? You know full well the idol is nothing."

"If it is nothing, Lord, why are you angry against it? If your children have worshiped nothing, why are you angry with them?"

At these words the face of God smiled and when Moses saw this smile he realized that God had forgiven. But the Lord said to him, "I have sworn, *The idolater shall die;* I cannot deny my oath; I have vowed to lead Israel no more; I cannot deny my vow."

Then, according to Rabbi Berechiah, Moses replied, "King of the World, did you not tell me that you obeyed your Torah, for those who command in the name of the law must first submit themselves to the law? Have you not, in your law, ordained, 'If any swear upon oath, they must accomplish all that their mouth has uttered, but a sage may set them free from their oath?' "

God replied to him, "Are you the sage, my son, who shall free me from my oath."

It is for this, according to our rabbis, that it is written: *Moses sat upon the mount,* for how could Moses have sat down before

God if it had not been to free him from his oath? He sat down, wrapped in his mantle, and God, standing before him, said unto him, "I have sworn to lead Israel no more, I have vowed Israel to death. I repent my oath; I regret my vow."

Moses, blessing the Lord, answered him, "The oath is no more, the vow has ceased."

It is for this, according to our rabbis, that it is written: *Moses, the man of God.* Moses was the man of God because he freed God from his oath.

When Moses saw that the Lord had forgiven Israel, he was sorry he had shattered the Torah. But the eternal said to him, "Be comforted, I will give you back the Torah."

Like a king who writes anew the torn-up contract when he takes back the wife he has put away, he rewrote before Moses the whole Torah. The first Torah had been written on high, on the sapphire of heaven; the second was written on earth, on earth's granite. This is why, say our sages, "The Torah speaks the language of humans; it is no longer in heaven, it is on earth."

For 40 days, in fasting, in prayer and in repentance, the children of Israel waited for the forgiveness of the Lord. The day on which the Torah, as the sign of forgiveness, was given back to them by the Lord was the tenth of the month of Tishri. God commanded Moses, "Let this day be remembered by you as a day of forgiveness, and not only by you and your children but also by your children's children in the generations that lie ahead."

So each year this day is, in this world, observed as the day of forgiveness for all in Israel, the day upon which the world is established and which shall continue even in the next world, when all the days of the world shall be blotted out.

Thus did the Tables of granite succeed the Tables of sapphire and the forgiveness of the Lord the sin of the golden calf. If the children of Israel had not worshiped the golden calf in the wilderness, they would have studied the sapphire Torah in the land of their ancestors to the end of days, but because they worshiped the golden calf in the wilderness, in mourning and in exile to the end of days will they study the granite Torah. For, our sages say, every sin of Israel is a remainder of the sin of the golden calf and in every generation in Israel there remains an ounce of the gold of the golden calf.

CHAPTER XIII

THE GLORY OF THE TABERNACLE

It is written, *I will dwell among them.* On this our teachers comment that when God had forgiven the Israelites for the adoration of the golden calf, they could not believe he had forgiven them. The angels had taken back from them the belts and crowns of glory that they had received at the word of the Lord, and now they, who once had looked face to face upon the splendor of the Lord, could not even look without lowering their eyes on the reflection which, unknown to him, shone upon Moses' face.

Then the Prophet said to the Holy One, blessèd be he, "King of the World, I know that you have forgiven them, but they do not know it and the world does not know it."

"As sure as you live," the Lord answered, "they will know it and the world will know it, for to prove it I will dwell among them. Thus, make me a sanctuary among the children of Israel. There they shall bring me their offerings and the redemption of their sins."

At these words Moses trembled, "How am I to make you, Lord, a sanctuary great enough for you to dwell among us? Can the whole world contain you?"

"I ask of you according to your ability, not mine," God answered. "On the north side 20 boards will be sufficient and 20 on the south and six toward the east and six toward the west, for my greatness can, when I will, enclose the infinite, and when I will, it can be enclosed in nothingness.

"How, Lord, bring you offerings? Could all the fruits of all the orchards, all the beasts of all the stalls, satisfy you?"

"I ask of you according to your ability, not mine," God answered. "A lamb in the morning and a lamb in the evening will be sufficient, and you shall eat its flesh. For God does not regard the burnt offering, but the willing heart that offereth it."

"How, Lord, shall we pay for our sins? For are not you, the ruler of all riches, poorer in riches than we are rich in sin?"

"I ask of you according to your ability, not mine," God answered. "The smallest coin of the basest metal in the purse of the poor will satisfy me, if you repent and make amends for your faults, for it is not enough to be pure before God, you must be pure before your neighbor also."

So Moses assembled the congregation of Israel and said to them, "God has forgiven you, but since you perceive him as far off, he now would give you his presence. Do not earthly rulers have palaces where their table is set, their torches lighted, their throne established? Should the Lord not have, like them, his palace on earth as a witness that he is our King and the King of all the earth? Surely the Holy One, blessèd be he, has no need of such. How can he who feeds all the world need a table set before him? Or torches, who lights the universe? Or a throne among you, who is enthroned throughout all space? Though he has no need of these, he will accept them as the witness of your love.

"When parents have children they care for them and feed them and clothe them and shelter them until they are grown up, and when the parents have grown old, the children, in turn, care for their parents and feed them and clothe and shelter them. God has treated you as children until this day; treat him now as a father and he, by accepting your unneeded gifts, will show to all the world that you are his children.

"Bring me thus cedar and skins of beasts and veils of blue and purple and scarlet to make him a sanctuary, and also gold and silver and brass and jewels and oil and spices and balm and sweet incense. You will offer him but what already is his, yet each of your offerings, however near to you it be, shall be as precious in his eyes as if you had brought it from the end of the world. When the Tabernacle is made, the Holy One, blessèd be he, who dwelt with the Torah in heaven among the angels, will with his Torah inhabit the earth and dwell among you."

Consider, say our teachers, how strange is the race of the children of Israel who rightly are compared to the dust of the earth and the stars of heaven. These same Hebrews who before had broken up for the idol their nose rings, now broke up for the Tabernacle their nose rings and their earrings and their finger rings, their seals and their necklaces; expiating five times, by the gold of the Tabernacle, the gold of the golden calf. Not content in their zeal to lavish their own gems, they seized and presented the jewels of their wives. But their wives, in yet more fervent zeal, came to Moses bringing myrrh and ointment and perfumes of every kind, diamonds and pearls and the precious stones of every land and purple and fine linen and costly stuffs of every color.

As the Prophet hesitated to accept them, they said to him, "If you will not receive of us what we have received of our husbands, let them give it to you in our names, but here are our mirrors of bronze, they are ours wholly; receive them of us."

At these words Moses was about to chase them out, crying, "Should I profane things holy by these things of lustful desire?"

But God said to him, "Do you not know that I myself did dress Eve's hair so the first woman might be more pleasing to the first man? Surely these mirrors which they bring you are dearer to me than the treasure of kings, for to them I owe my people. When they were in Egypt and returned to their homes after the toil of their bondage, their wives gave them meat and drink; then they drew out their mirrors and therein mirrored their faces side-by-side and said to them as they caressed them, 'Behold—you are fair and

I am fairer than you.' Then forgetting their bondage and coupling with their wives in the joy of their flesh, they multiplied the children and the souls of Israel. Thus accept these mirrors of the desire that is sanctified by human love and out of them make the basin for pure water that shall sanctify my priests in my love."

The riches of the camp piled up before Moses. So great was their ardor that after two days the Prophet had to announce that God wanted no more and when on the third day the prince of the tribes came with their gifts, he refused them. The People had given too much. Thus, say our sages, the children of Israel returned to their Father what they had received from him, but he, in the end of time, shall give it back to them, for then, through all Eternity, they shall be sustained in his glory and clothed in his glory beneath the Tabernacle of his glory.

When Moses had gathered up all this treasure he asked the Holy One, blessèd be he, "How shall I make your sanctuary?"

The Holy One answered him, "Have I not shown it you in heaven? All that is on high must be on earth. Make my dwelling place on earth like that on high."

"Am I a god, to make it so?"

"Behold, the Book of the Generations of Adam. In it are written the destinies of every mortal, from the birth of living things to the resurrection of the dead. Here you will find the name of the one whom I have named by name to build my sanctuary."

Moses read and found the name: it was Bezalel, the son of Hur whom the Israelites had killed when he sought to stop them from making the idol. Because Hur had died in order that the idol should not be made, God had chosen Bezalel, his son, to make the Tabernacle and Solomon, the son of his sons, to make the Temple. Bezalel, like Solomon after him, was filled with the spirit of wisdom and understanding. His name signifies "In the shadow of God." As it is written, *A good name is better than precious ointment* for, say our rabbis, where does the perfume of precious ointment go? From the sleeping chamber unto the feasting chamber, but a good name goes from one end of the world to the other.

When Moses chose, according to the Lord's choice, the name of Bezalel, God said, "Does Bezalel seem capable for the task?"

"He is acceptable to me, King of the World, if he is to you."

"Nevertheless, go ask the children of Israel if he seems good to them," the Lord said to him.

The Prophet questioned them. They answered, "He is acceptable to us, if he is acceptable to God and to you."

Beside Bezalel, who was of the tribe of Judah, Moses placed Oholiab, of the tribe of Dan for, says Rabbi Hanina ben Pazzi, there is nothing greater than Judah nor anything smaller than Dan, but there is neither great nor small in the eye of the eternal.

Thus Moses commanded Bezalel to make the Tabernacle. Bezalel asked him, "Moses, our master, why make a Tabernacle?"

"To receive within it the Torah."

"But where shall we set the Torah?"

"When you have made the Tabernacle, you shall make the Ark for the Torah."

"Is it good that the Torah should await, unhoused, the house of the Tabernacle? Let us first make the Ark for the Torah, then the Tabernacle."

"Truly," said the Prophet, "you do merit your name for by your wisdom you live in the shadow of God."

So Bezalel began with the Ark for the Torah, which is Light; thus following the example of God who created Light before anything else at the Creation. The Ark had to be of great beauty for it is like that king, Rabbi Judah bar Ilai says, who having a most beautiful daughter, commanded saying, "Make for my daughter a beautiful throne so that by her throne shall her beauty be known." In the same way the Lord commanded Moses, "Make for my daughter, the Torah, a beautiful Ark so that by her Ark shall her beauty be known."

Rabbi Hanina and Resh Lakish were not of the same opinion as to the coffers of the Ark. According to Rabbi Hanina it was made of three coffers: one of gold, inside which Bezalel put one of cedar, inside which he put another of gold. According to Resh Lakish it was made of a single coffer of cedar which Bezalel overlaid with gold within and without.

Above the Ark he set the Cherubim of gold. Each measured one span and had each two wings, measuring ten spans, the whole corresponding to the 22 letters of the divine alphabet used to write the Torah and to create, through the Torah, heaven and earth.

It was from between the two Cherubim set upon the Ark that the presence of God spoke from then on to Moses, for not for any human, not even Moses, has the presence of God ever come quite down to earth as likewise for God no human, not even Moses, has ever gone quite up to the most high place in heaven. These Cherubim were two in number, one for Elohim who is justice, the other for Adonai who is mercy, for mercy and justice are the two faces of the Lord. These two faces were half turned away from each other, but when Israel was united in love and peace, they turned and faced one another and their looking and their lips were made one in their kissing for, as it is written in the holy Zohar,[1] *When man is at one, God is One.*

In the sanctuary on high Moses had seen a table and a candlestick in front of the Throne of splendor. He was able to remember the table and could paint it in words for Bezalel, who made one like it of cedar wood overlaid with gold, with a border of gold around it. This table, in remembrance of the feasting of the Righteous in the Garden of Eden, had on it twelve loaves of bread

---

[1] *The Book of the Splendor,* the best known of the many books of the Kabbala. —*Trans.*

to recall the twelve months of the year that the sun sustains and the twelve tribes of Israel that sustain the Lord God.

But Moses could not remember the candlestick to paint it in words. He returned to God who showed it to him—made of white fire and red fire and green fire and black fire. Scarcely had he come down before once again he had forgotten, and twice again this happened. Finally God said, "Command Bezalel to make the candlestick; he will do it."

At once, without speaking a word, Bezalel made it, with its golden lilies and golden fruits and seven golden branches, each of which, lighting a flame, was to recall the seven days that their round lights up in the week and the seven stars that their round lights in heaven. When the candlestick was made, Moses said to Bezalel, "I saw it three times and three times forgot it; you, without having seen it, have remembered it. Glory, Bezalel, to your art, the shadow of the eternal, which creates for the eternal the shadow of his light."

Then he commanded Bezalel to make two altars like those he had seen in the sanctuary on high—one for burnt offerings, in reminder of the human body, the other for incense, in reminder of the human soul. The altar of burnt offerings was of brass, the incense altar of gold, for the soul is more precious than the body, but both served each day, for each day people must serve God with their whole soul and with their whole body.

When these works were done, Bezalel and Oholiab, with their wise-hearted workers, began the Tabernacle. But of all the skins of beasts, only the skin of the tahash,[2] which is 30 cubits long, sufficed for the curtains of the Tabernacle, and of all the kinds of cedar only the cedar of Shittim that excels among all cedars would suffice for the planks of the Tabernacle. When the cedars of Shittim had been brought for the planks of the Tabernacle the cedars began to sing, and when the skins of the tahash had been brought

[2] A species of seal. —*Trans.*

for the curtains of the Tabernacle the tahash disappeared from the world. After Bezalel and Oholiab formed and set up the planks, then they designed and set up the curtains.

The Tabernacle was 70 cubits long because of the 70 nations of the earth and it had 70 curtains because of the 70 names of Israel. It contained 70 vessels because of the 70 names of the Lord, for it was to unite the nations with Israel and Israel with the Lord.

Thus was the whole work of the Tabernacle, created by the art of Bezalel, like the whole work of the six days created by the Creator: the double stone of the Torah set in the Ark was like heaven and earth set in the void on the First Day; the blue veil divided the Holy One from the Holy of Holies as the firmament divided the waters above from the waters below on the Second Day; the golden table bore the pure wheat as the earth had born grass, the herb yielding seed and the fruit tree giving fruit, on the Third Day; the golden candlestick bore its flames as the lights had born light upon the Fourth Day; the Cherubim with their wings flew like the birds on the Fifth Day; and as humans had been created in Eden in the image of God so on the Sixth Day the priest in the sanctuary was to purify the image of humans before the face of God to the End of Days. This is why, our sages say, before the Tabernacle the world was still unfirm and the creation of the Tabernacle was to make firm the Creation.

But the work of Bezalel and Oholiab and their wise-hearted workers was not yet finished before the children of Israel began murmuring against the Prophet yet again. When he rose up early, the Israelites, so says Rabbi Hija, said behind his back, "Behold the son of Amram, who rises early to get in his provision of manna before us and take the best from us." When he rose up late, the Israelites said before his face, "Behold the son of Amram, who rises late; he ate too much manna last night; neither his wife nor his son have been able to wake him." When he walked among the multitude in his great humility, the Israelites pointed at him nearby saying, "Behold the son of Amram, how he walks among us, that we may bow to him." When, in his humility, he held himself aloof, the Israelites pointed at him afar, saying, "Behold the son of Amram, how he holds himself aloof, to make it plain that he is greater than we."

According to Rabbi Hama, Dathan and other slanderers went everywhere saying, "You brought him your brass and silver, gold and jewels, but have you received an account for them? This dreamer was not rich before the Tabernacle, nor will he be poor after."

All cried, "Let him be accountable! Let him be accountable!"

Thus Moses, having assembled them, listed all that he had received and spent. But Korah, Pharaoh's former treasurer, who could compute more quickly than the rest, rose up and cried, "There are 1,775 shekels missing!"

That sum actually was missing and the mob was already howling at him savagely when, before their eyes, the rivets that Oholiab and Bezalel had nailed to the staves of the Tabernacle began to flash like a multitude of stars—they were the 1,775 shekels that the Prophet had not counted. Korah had to cease from his lying insults and the multitude had to bow down.

In the month of Kislev when the work of Oholiab and Bezalel and their wise-hearted workers was finished, the muttering broke forth anew. It was not enough to have assembled the Tabernacle, it had now to be raised up. But God did not will that his presence should descend into it until the anniversary of the birth of Isaac, whom Abraham had offered to the Lord upon the rock Moriah, Israel's first altar.

Certain of the people who did not know this sought out the wise-hearted workers who had helped Oholiab and Bezalel and said to them, "Why are you idle, you slothful! Raise up the Tabernacle, that God may come down into it." But the workmen could not raise it up. Then the people sought out Bezalel and Oholiab and said to them, "You slothful, why are you idle? Raise up the Tabernacle, that God may come down into it." But neither Oholiab nor Bezalel could raise it up.

Then the Israelites came to Moses, crying, "You commanded us to bring you cedar wood, skins of beasts, veils of purple, scarlet, crimson and blue, brass, silver, gold and jewels, oil and spices and balm and sweet incenses. Have we refused you anything? What good does the Tabernacle do us if they who have made it cannot raise it up? You told us, 'God will come down among you.' Did you lie, then? Had God not promised it to you? Then for whom have you taken our all from us? For him, or for yourself?"

Moses asked the Lord, "What am I to answer them, King of the World? Why do you not will that the Tabernacle be raised up?"

The eternal answered him, "Moses, my son, I have read in your heart that you were grieved to have no part in the building of my sanctuary: the children of Israel furnished the 13 materials; Oholiab and Bezalel have assembled them, but I have wanted to show to everyone that the offerings of all and the work of all would be nothing without you. Now go, raise up the Tabernacle."

"How can I, Lord?"

"Go, you shall do it."

It came to pass when Moses touched the Tabernacle as it lay vast upon the ground, by itself the Tabernacle rose up and when, like the world with its firmament and its mountains and its plains and its seas, it was wholly risen up, then the altar of the body and the altar of the soul and the table for bread and the basin for water and the candlestick of stars—all, by themselves, went in and ranged themselves with the Throne of the Torah. All the children of Israel cried, "Blessèd be the Lord God who blesses Moses."

CHAPTER XIV

THE DAY OF THE TEN CROWNS

The Tabernacle was raised, but the splendor of God did not yet inhabit it. See how modest was Moses? Just as he had not gone up to the burning bush until the Lord had called him, so he would not enter the Tabernacle until he had received from the Lord a sign. He pondered in his heart, "Is it I, or another, whom he will choose for his High Priest?"

Then Abiram the scoffer renewed his scoffing, "The Tabernacle is reared, but where is God? We were promised his presence. Can you see it? I cannot."

Moses answered; "In order that the Holy One, blessèd be he, descend among you, you must be purified by one who has no impurity."

As he was asking himself who this pure one would be, the Lord commanded him, "Number your Israelites from 20 years old and upwards and let each bring you a half shekel for the redemption of his soul, but you shall not number the tribe of Levi among the children of Israel and you shall count Joseph as two tribes—in the names of his sons, Ephraim and Manasseh."

"Why number them, King of the World?" the Prophet questioned him, "You have 70 nations in the world and you do not command me to number them."

"All are my nations, "the Lord answered him, "but Israel is my flock, and, like the shepherd whose sheep a wolf has chased, so must I know what remains unto me."

Everyone brought a half shekel for the aid of the Tabernacle and Moses numbered them. There were 600,000 less 3,000, for the Israelites were 603,000 when they left Egypt, but 3,000 had died by the sin of the golden calf and 3,000 by the pestilence that came after the sin of the golden calf. In this way the children of Israel shall be numbered in the last days, but no mortal will know the sum for then all their souls will be redeemed and God alone will be able to number them, as it is written, *They shall be more numerous than the sands of the sea and the stars of the heaven.*

When the Israelites had been numbered, Abiram the scoffer still scoffed, saying, "Now we cannot see God, to the number of 603,000 less 3,000."

Then the eternal commanded Moses, "Put apart the lepers among the people." For after the Lord had forgiven Israel the sin of the golden calf, the pestilence that kills had disappeared, but leprosy, that does not kill, had not disappeared.

Ten, says Rabbi Judah bar Shalom, are the causes of leprosy: pride and ambition, calumny and lying, theft, murder and fornication, profaning the divine name, blasphemy and idolatry. This is why leprosy remained on the body, as sin upon the soul, of Israel.

Moses thus commanded that the lepers should be put outside the camp. This ordinance was always a law in Israel. When the lepers were divided from the Israelites, Abiram the scoffer did not cease his scoffing, "Now I can see no lepers, but I still cannot see God."

Then the eternal said to Moses, "Now number the sons of Levi from one month old and upwards. Let every firstborn among the children of Israel bring to the sons of Levi five shekels for the redemption of the firstborn, for if the children of Israel had kept in their flesh the seal of my covenant in Egypt and had not worshiped the golden calf in the wilderness, the firstborn of Israel would have kept my sanctuary. Because the children of Levi alone kept upon their flesh the seal of my covenant in Egypt and alone did not in the wilderness worship the golden calf, they alone in the place of the firstborn of Israel shall keep my sanctuary. It is for this that each firstborn of Israel shall redeem himself from each son of Levi. Then you shall number separately each family in Levi by their names, the families of Kohath and of Gershon and of Merari, for I will choose from among the sons of Levi the pure one who shall be the priest among my priests and shall purify before my face my people among the peoples."

Moses had trembled when he had been commanded not to number them of Levi, but to number them of Israel. He was a son of Levi and he thought in his heart, "Is there a blot upon the sons of Levi?" But when he heard God set in his love those of Kohath above those of Gershon who were the firstborn in the order of their birth, he rejoiced; he was a son of Kohath and he thought in his heart, "God will choose me from among those of Kohath as priest among his priests."

When he had numbered all the sons of Levi, family by family, there were 22,300. Each of the firstborn of the tribe of Jacob brought them five shekels for the redemption of the firstborn, for it was for five shekels that the sons of Jacob had sold their brother. Then the Elders of Israel laid their hands upon all those of Levi, making of each a firstborn of Israel. But Abiram and the scoffers cried out upon him, "Can your firstborn see God better than if they had never been born?"

Then the eternal commanded Moses, "Take from among the descendants of Levi those who have come to years of understanding; take them apart from the Israelites near the Tabernacle and for seven days instruct them, according to the laws of my Torah, in the things my Torah expects of them."

For seven days Moses taught them. He showed them the burnt offering and the peace offering; the offering for the sin sinned wittingly and the offering for the sin sinned in ignorance; that of the Sabbath and of each day and of each month; of the Passover which is in memory of the going up out of Egypt; of Shabuoth[1] which is to recall the gift upon Sinai; the offering for Kippur[2] which, with the fast, is in memory of the forgiveness; and the offering of Succoth[3] which, with the booths of branches, is for the joy of Israel in the tents of the wilderness.

In these sacrificial offerings sheep or goats, lambs or bulls are offered up with the offerings of wine and oil and flour. These beasts are clean and others unclean. Why, ask our rabbis, sacrifice beasts? Does God, who has forbidden us the blood of animals lest we become bloodthirsty, eat their flesh or drink their blood? And why sacrifice not the unclean but the clean beasts? It is because humans may eat only the clean beasts and sacrifice to God only the clean beasts of which they may eat, for God does not desire food for himself, but rather humans when they are fed shall feel themselves fed by God. This is why since the destruction of the Temple the recital of the sacrifice has served as sacrifice.

He also showed them the incense made with the 13 perfumes from the gardens of the earth and the isles of the sea to dissolve into the air at the touch of fire which in its four forms gives back the creation to the Creator and, rejoicing the heart of people, rejoices also the heart of God.

Beyond this he taught them the 18 benedictions and all the prayers and among the prayers the most sacred of all prayers, the *Shema*, for as it is written in the Zohar, when Israel proclaims in

[1] Shabuoth, the Feast of Weeks.

[2] Yom Kippur, the Day of Atonement.

[3] Succoth, the Feast of Tabernacles.

this world, *Hear, O Israel, the Lord is our God, the Lord is One*[4] the Oneness of God is perfected in this world and in all the worlds.

Then he taught them the chanting of prayer. This chanting must never stop for when Israel on earth ceases from its chanting, the song of the angels on high ceases also.

Moses made all the Levites put on the four Levitical vestments: the narrow breeches of fine twined linen that atone for concupiscence; the straight miter of fine linen that atones for theft; the coat without fold or color or blemish that atones for bloodshed. Then he took a single measure of oil to anoint them and mingled it with myrrh, saffron, cinnamon and balm. Such was the purity of that single measure of oil that for 2,000 years it sufficed to sanctify all the Levites, all the Kings and all the High Priests in Israel.

God said to Moses, "I know that in your heart you wish to be my High Priest. But because you lifted up your hammer against Aaron when you thought he had served the idol, Aaron shall be my High Priest. And to show your humility before all, proclaim before all that I have chosen him."

When Moses proclaimed the greatness of his brother before the people, according to God's will, Aaron trembled. The horns of the altar reminded him of the horns of the golden calf and however sure his innocence, he did not feel sure that he was innocent.

He said, "How can it be, Moses, that you have had all the toil and I shall have all the reward?"

Moses answered, "My labor was yours. Your reward shall be mine."

Thus, say our rabbis, Aaron and Moses were for Israel like the twin breasts of a woman. Aaron and Moses made the beauty of Israel. As the two breasts nourish the child with milk, Moses and Aaron nourished Israel with love.

---

[4] In the Authorized Version of the Bible: *Hear, O Israel: the Lord thy God is One Lord.* Several renderings are possible, but that chosen is perhaps nearest the Jewish conception. —*Trans.*

But Abiram cried, "I see a doubled Moses, but I do not see God." And the scoffers laughed with him.

The Prophet, without paying attention to them, said before the assembly, "Blessed be Aaron whom the Lord has chosen for his High Priest!" He taught him the divination of the stones on which are the twelve names of the tribes, whose twelve gleaming lights reveal Israel's future. He taught him the laying on of hands upon the scapegoat that bears away into the wilderness Israel's past.

Then giving his brother, who was already clad in the four vestments of the Levite, the four vestments of the High Priest, he said to him, "Gird on the blue coat bordered with bells that atones for calumny; gird on the vestment of gold cloth that atones for idolatry; gird on the double breastplate that atones for forfeiture; gird on the triple crown that atones for blasphemy. Behold, God has clothed you like an angel for when your heart is sanctified beneath your sanctified vestments, and by the righteousness of the Patriarchs sanctifying Israel and the world, you shall enter the Holy of Holies, where the angels are, he desires that you shall be like an angel. Now by this oil with which I anoint your head and the heads of your sons, I pour out the gifts of the priestly power for the ages that shall follow after the ages, upon you and upon your sons and upon your sons' sons." Then, turning toward the congregation, he said to them, "Be pure even as God is pure. He will dwell among you if he finds in your pure hearts a Tabernacle."

But Abiram cried, "I had my heart before so why your Tabernacle?"

Now the day approached upon which God planned to make his presence manifest and lasting. The princes of the tribes brought to the completed sanctuary the gifts that had been too late for the sanctuary's beginning. Together they offered six covered wagons of brass and twelve oxen without blemish for the carrying of the holy dwelling place. For the feasts of the dedication each offered a spoon of ten shekels in gold filled with incense, a silver charger of 130 shekels' weight, a silver bowl of 70 shekels filled with flour kneaded in oil for the oblation, a bullock, a lamb and a ram of the first year for the burnt offering, a kid for the sin offering and for the peace offering two bulls, five rams, five goats and five yearling lambs. The Prophet, after consulting God, accepted them and all in Israel and all in Levi walked in procession to the Tabernacle behind Moses and Aaron with Nadab and Abihu and Eleazar and Ithamar, the sons of Aaron, to see the splendor of the Lord come down before the face of the multitude.

This day, the first of the month of Nisan, was crowned with ten crowns. It was the first of the week, the first of the month, the first of the year; the first day on which the princes of the tribes brought their offerings and the first on which the Levites went in to sing their songs and sacrifice and eat their part of the burnt offering. For the first time the altar would light up with fire, Aaron would bless Israel and the Tabernacle would be blessed with the glory of the Lord.

On that day the happiest among all women was Elisheba, daughter of Amminadab. Her brother Nahshon was prince of his tribe, her brother-in-law Moses was the Prophet, her sons Eleazar, Ithamar, Nadab and Abihu were chief of the priests and Aaron, her spouse, High Priest. But days, like kings, lose their crowns.

"Mend your ways on the eve of your death," Rabbi Eleazar used to say.

"But," his disciple answered him, "can I tell on what day I shall die?"

"True, you do not know it, so mend your ways each day."

But Nadab and Abihu had in no way mended their ways, and they did not know they were about to die, and their mother did not know that they were about to die.

Ceaselessly they chanted in their pride, "The brother of our mother is prince of his tribe. The brother of our father is the

Prophet. We are chiefs of the priests and our father, High Priest. What daughter of Israel could be good enough for us?"

As they walked in the procession behind Moses and Aaron, Abihu said to Nadab, "When shall we be chief in Israel?"

Nadab replied, "When these two old men shall die."

The Holy One, blessèd be he, who seeks the offering of the pure in heart, heard them. But, according to our rabbis, his mercy which forgives breathes in every hour of the day, and his justice which chastises breathes only in a thousandth part of a thousandth part of a second each day. So that this time yet again he forgave.

All Israel was assembled before the altar set before the sanctuary. By a miracle of God this space, measuring six seahs, easily contained 60 hosts of grown men and as many youth. Thus also when the Lord appears for the Last Judgment all the dead shall rise, from Adam to his last posterity, and Zion, without increasing in space, shall be vast enough to hold their whole multitude.

The wood was set upon the altar and the victim was set upon the wood. This victim was a bullock to atone for the sin of the golden calf. Aaron, turning toward the congregation, pronounced the blessing of the high priest upon them, "The Lord bless you and keep you. The Lord make his face to shine upon you and be gracious unto you. The Lord lift up his countenance upon you and give you peace." And all awaited the presence of the Lord, but it came not.

Then Aaron entered into the sanctuary to pray, but though he prayed God was still absent. Aaron thought in his heart, "Why is not Moses the high priest? The Holy One, blessèd be he, is angry with me. My sin hides from him his servant who should hide from him the sin of Israel."

As he was praying Moses rejoined him in the Tabernacle and together they entered into the Holy of Holies. While their united prayers rose up to the Cherubim, the eyes and the mouths of the

Cherubim united and before the multitude a fire from God fell upon the altar, a flame rose up and consumed the offering and a smoke rose up bearing it to heaven. Of such kind was this fire that it burned for centuries without melting or tarnishing the brass of the altar. Of such kind was the smoke that it smoked for centuries, rising as straight in all winds as if it had been granite.

When all the people saw this, they felt the presence of God among them and fell on their faces and sang to the Lord. The Lord also was joyful, for, says Rabbi Samuel bar Abba, the Holy One, blessèd be he, wishes to dwell on earth. The sin of Adam banished him out of it. By the grace of Moses he inhabited it again. His Creation, till then unsteady, at last rested as on a firmly set tripod on its three golden pedestals—Love, Law and Sacrifice.

While all Israel was now but one cleansed heart before God, Nadab and Abihu without having purified their flesh in the ritual bath nor having put sanctified fire in their censers, had their heads and their hearts full of the strong wine of their pride. They followed Moses and Aaron into the sanctuary and when they found them praying in the Holy of Holies, Nadab said to Abihu, "When shall we be chief in Israel?"

Abihu answered him, "When shall these two old men die?"

As this was the moment of the second when justice breathes, it hurled forth their punishment. The two Cherubim divided their mouths; their two faces turned away from each other. The eyes of one of them flashed two lightning bolts and from each bolt came forth two more bolts, long and fine as two threads of gold. The four lightning bolts entered, invisible, into the four nostrils of the two sinners and without a sound, without a cry, in their unscathed bodies, their souls were consumed.

Elisheba lamented sorrowfully! Utterly mute was Aaron! He took no part in their funeral rites, since sight of the dead is a defilement to the High Priest whose spirit must turn toward the

Only Living. But great was the grief of his heart and he reproached himself because of his grief, thinking, "All the princes of the tribes have offered to God an offering according to his wish. Levi alone has offered nothing and I am prince of Levi. Has my grief turned me then aside from the Lord and made me unfit to offer him anything?"

Then Moses said to him, "Light the lamps of the candlestick. You shall offer to God the light of the sanctuary."

Why, ask our rabbis, did the Holy One, blessèd be he, desire that the light should be lighted up before him? It is like that man who had sight and who had traveled with a blind man, guiding him all along the road. In the evening when they came to their resting place, he said to the blind man, "Light the torch for me." Did the blind man need to see? In no way. But he did not wish that any one should be able to say that he had done everything for the blind man and that for him the blind man had done nothing. God is the man with sight, Israel the blind. God desires that the peoples shall say of Israel, "Behold! Israel lights the Lord." For if the peoples had known what salvation to the world the Tabernacle would be, they would themselves have built the Tabernacle. If they had known what salvation to the world would be the light of the Tabernacle, they would themselves have lighted its light.

When Aaron had lighted the lamps, the golden candlestick lighted the world and beneath the serene sky, for Aaron's sake showing his presence to the world, the glory of the Lord came down to inhabit, in a cloud of glory, the glory of the sanctuary.

CHAPTER XV

MOSES, OUR MASTER

From the day when the presence of God came to dwell in the Tabernacle, the word of the Lord came to the Prophet in a new form. Until then the Holy One, blessèd be he, had spoken to him as through a vast trumpet and Moses' face could be seen to redden when he heard it.

Now the voice of the eternal was so gentle, so constant and intimate, that not only could it not be heard either by humans or by angels, it was no longer revealed by any troubling of the Prophet's face.

This voice murmured to him, "Formerly there was enmity between me and my children and anger and hate. Now there is friendship and peace and love."

The Prophet answered, "King of the World, since now there is union between you and your people, since your presence in the cloud of glory repulses from them the evil spirits of demons and the evil eye of the nations, since I have built for them your Tabernacle and for them set your Torah in your Tabernacle, is not my task completed?"

"No, my son. What is my love for my people, if my people do not know how to preserve it? What is my Torah for my people if they do not know how to practice it? Since you have set for them my Torah in my Tabernacle, now teach them my Torah. Let them practice it and preserve my love."

From that day forth Moses, our master, taught the Torah to the children of Israel.

This, according to our rabbis, is how he taught it: Aaron came first to receive the word of God, then the two sons of Aaron, Eleazar and Ithamar, who received it in their turn while Aaron listened, seated upon the right hand of Moses. Then the Prophet instructed the elders while Eleazar listened, seated on his father's right and Ithamar listened, seated on Moses' left. Finally they of the people came up to be instructed equally with the high priest.

When Moses ended, he withdrew. Then Aaron repeated what he had learned, then Eleazar and Ithamar his sons, then all the others, until everyone, from the first to the last, had said over their lesson four times, for the eternal commanded Moses to implant his Torah four times in the children of Israel.

He said to them what our sages have since repeated, "The study of the Torah is worth more than sacrificial offerings and more than incense. When three people eating at the same table do not speak of the Torah, it is as though they ate of a meal offered up to an idol. But when three people eating at the same table speak to one another of the Torah, it is as though they ate at the Lord's table. Thus seek out the Torah, for it will not come to seek you. If you do not seek it in your youth, how shall you find it in your maturity? But when you have found it, do not attribute any merit to yourselves, for God has created you for the Torah."

And he said to them another time, "Behold the ten commandments written on the two tables that I received from the eternal. They make but one commandment, for each of them, on one of the tables, answers one of the others, upon the other table.

"The first that says, *I am the Lord your God*, faces the sixth, *You shall not kill*, for the murderer destroys God's image.

"The second, *You shall have no other gods before me*, faces the seventh, *You shall not commit adultery*, for idolatry is one infidelity and adultery is another no less sinful.

"The third, *You shall not take the name of the Lord your God in vain,* faces the eighth, *You shall not steal,* for blasphemy is a theft from God and theft leads to blasphemy.

"*You shall not bear false witness against your neighbor* faces *Remember the Sabbath to keep it holy,* for the one who breaks the Sabbath, forgetting that in six days the Lord made heaven and earth and rested the seventh day, is a false witness against the Lord.

"*Honor your father and your mother* faces *you shall not covet,* for those who covet that which they do not have, do not relish what they have and do not honor them who have given it unto them.

"Such is the union between these commandments that they who break the last, break them all, for they that covet, covet other gods and other parents and rebel against God and worship other gods and sanctify not any day and bear witness against themselves and in their thoughts steal and kill and in their hearts commit adultery."

Thus Moses explained to them the laws they had already received; then he taught them those they did not yet know:

You shall break down the house, when the leprosy spreads within it....

You shall not stew the kid in its mother's milk....

You shall not lend with interest to your relative....

You shall restore what a poor person has hocked at sunset so that they may sleep in their cloak....

If anyone injures the eye of a servant, that person shall let the servant go free, for the eye's sake....

If a Hebrew, your kin, be sold to you, that one shall serve you six years and in the seventh year you shall let that person go free and with gifts, for you were a slave in the land of Egypt and the Lord your God redeemed you....

You shall not plow with an ox and an ass yoked together....

You shall not muzzle the ox when it grinds out the corn....

When you reap the harvest of your land, you shall not entirely reap the corners of your field, neither shall you gather the gleaning of your harvest; you shall leave this part for the poor and for the foreigner, for the widow and the orphan, for the Lord your God supports the orphan and the widow and loves the foreigner; thus you shall love the foreigner; for you were foreigners in the land of Egypt.

Sometimes those who listened to Moses questioned him.

Jethro the proselyte said to him, "Moses, our master, it is written in your Torah, *I am a jealous God, visiting the iniquity of the parents upon the children unto the third and fourth generation;* and it is written in the Torah, *The children shall not be put to death for the parents, for no one shall be put to death except for their own sin.* Are there then two laws in your law?"

And Moses answered him, "It is written, *I visit the iniquity of the parents upon the children,* for God wants the parents to recoil from those sins with which anyone would reproach their children. It is written, *No one shall be put to death except for their own sin,* because God does not want the innocent to pay for the guilty."

Joshua the disciple said to him, "Moses, our master, it is written in your Torah, *You shall love your neighbor as yourself;* and it is also written in your Torah, *An eye for an eye and a tooth for a tooth.* Is it love of your neighbors to demand of them their eye or their tooth?"

Moses answered him, "It is written, *You shall love your neighbor as yourself,* for the name of the Lord is Love. And it is written, *An eye for an eye and a tooth for a tooth,* for it is against love to let the wicked go free and the wicked must expiate their faults to deserve love."

Korah the rich asked Moses, "Moses, our master, it is written in your Torah, *Take not from the poor, for they are poor.* Who can take from the poor, since they have nothing?"

And Moses answered him, "That which you should give to the poor belongs to them; that which you do not give the poor, you take from them."

While Moses at the foot of Sinai thus taught the Torah to the children of Israel, in the school of Heaven Zagzagel taught it to the angels and in the Garden of Eden the Holy One, blessèd be he, taught it to the righteous, who are above the angels.

The righteous in their turn questioned the Holy One. Abraham said to him, "King of the World, you have written in your Torah, *In the beginning God created heaven and earth.* Was there then already a beginning, when you created the world? And what did you do, in this beginning?"

According to Rabbi Abbahu, God answered, "Before the world that now is, I created other worlds and because they did not please me, I destroyed them."

Jacob asked the eternal, "King of the World, you have written in your Torah, *You shall not make unto you any graven image, nor any likeness of anything that is in heaven above, or that is in the earth beneath.* Since you rebuke the idolater, why do you not destroy what the idolater worshiped?"

God answered him, according to Rabban Gambiel, "They worship the sun, the moon, the stars, the mountains and the waters. Ought I to destroy the world because they cannot understand me?"

And Isaac asked the eternal, "King of the World, when you made the light, you said in your Torah that the light was good. When you made the expanse of the firmament and the expanse of the earth, you said in your Torah that they were good. Every herb you have made and every beast, you have said that they are good, but when you made humankind in your image, you did not say in your Torah that humans were good. Why, Lord?"

And God answered him, "Because I have not yet perfected humankind and because through the Torah humans are to perfect themselves and to perfect the world."

Our sages have said that to study the Torah without practicing it is equivalent to not knowing God. Thus Moses, in order to practice it and to have it practiced, judged the Israelites according to the Torah. Everyone brought their lawsuits to him, standing around him all day long. He, dressed exactly like the others and without any sign to distinguish him from any of them, seated upon his bench, listened to them and judged them, interpreting and applying the law—condemning sometimes, conciliating often.

But the people of Israel are a disputatious people; to gain one shekel they will expend 70. Was a litigant about to lose his cause? He announced new evidence, new witnesses and from week to week and from month to month he insisted upon adjournments. Did he lose? He accused Moses of twisting the law and of furnishing himself with arguments in the purse of his adversary.

Sometimes the Prophet chided them, "You stiff-necked people! When will you be content? How am I to bless you? How am I to support you? Let the Lord support you, let the Lord bless you!"

But they answered, "He has sworn that he will multiply us like the sands of the sea and the stars of heaven; we have no need of your benediction; your integrity would satisfy us."

For, our doctors comment, as the rooster among flying things or the dog among quadrupeds, so is the Israelite impudent among the nations and out of ten parts of effrontery that God has apportioned to the world, Israel has taken nine for itself. Thus Moses was surrounded with quarrelling and cries from morning to evening.

Seeing this, Jethro the proselyte said to him, "Moses, our master, if you continue like this you will not go far. May it please you to listen to my advice and to follow it, if God approve it.

Continue to be the interpreter of the revelation, repeating to the children of Israel the word that you receive from the eternal. Teach them to sacrifice, to praise, to keep the Sabbath and the feasts, to sanctify their marriages, to educate their children, to care for the sick, to bury the dead, to practice justice and sometimes to renounce justice in favor of love.

"But to judge them, choose from among them those of good reputation, whom you shall instruct and in whom there shall be wisdom, fear of the Lord, modesty, hatred of pretense and love of humankind and of truth. These people shall be judges over Israel and you shall be judge over these judges and let peace reign between the people and the judges and between the judges and yourself."

This counsel was pleasing in the eyes of the Prophet and it was pleasing to the Lord, for God, wishing this thing to be done, wanted it to be done through the advice of Jethro in order that in him the proselyte should be honored and that the proselyte should have honor in the Torah. This is why the Prophet, who could have hidden from posterity Jethro's part, in his modesty added a chapter to the Torah telling of the counsel of the proselyte and proclaiming his wisdom.

Moses, having assembled the children of Israel, said to them, "Choose from among you those to judge you and, from among these choices, I will choose you judges."

They did not delay to obey him, for each of them thought in their hearts, "Moses will name hosts of judges—judges of tens, judges of hundreds, judges of thousands. If I am not one of them, my child may be, or my grandchild, or the child of my sibling, or the spouse of my sibling, or the sibling of the spouse of my sibling, or my friend, or a friend of my friend, or the friend of the friend of a friend. And when that one is judge, a small present will incline this judge's justice to my side."

Moses was well aware of their thoughts and knew that an evil judge makes the balance of the whole world incline towards evil and that a good judge is as precious as the sum of all other good things. But not being able to find perfect ones, he chose the best among the least evil and said to them, "Blessed be you who are judged worthy to judge the children of Abraham, Isaac and Jacob, whom God himself has called his children. Notice how the high priest approaches the altar with short steps. In like manner go with short steps toward justice, for if justice be not prudent it is not just.

"If a rich person and a poor one come before you and right is on the side of the poor person, you shall not say, 'Why should I humble the rich who humble the poor?' But if the right is on the side of the rich you shall not say, 'The poor person has nothing, why should I impoverish the poor?'

"If a strong human and a weak come before you and right is on the side of the weak, you shall not say, 'Why should I get myself killed by the strong?' But if the right is on the side of the strong, you shall not say, 'Why should I let the strong kill the weak?'

"As the palm gives the date and the thorn, so a judge gives absolution and punishment, but if judges do not know how to punish, neither will they know how to absolve. If they do not know how to punish nor how to absolve, in no way will they shelter the world beneath the shade of peace."

And they went out and they judged Israel.

Now for more than a year Jethro the proselyte had dwelt beside Moses in the desert, learning from him the love of the Torah and the goodness of the Lord.

He said to the Prophet, "Moses, our master, let me return into Midian, which is my land and the land of my ancestors."

But Moses did not wish to let him go, for, according to Rabbi Meir, the idolater who learns the Torah is greater than Aaron the high priest.

He answered him, "Jethro, my master, why do you not remain among us? True it is that you shall have no part in the land that shall be given to us, for God does not desire that the proselyte, coming to the Lord, should seem to seek other recompense than to have found God. But your children and your grandchildren shall be like our children and our grandchildren.

"If you should leave us now, what would the other nations say? They would claim that Israel dismissed the father-in-law of its Prophet because he is but a foreigner, that Israel keeps its God for itself alone and that its God wishes to be the God of a single people.

"Remain then, you who enlighten the one whom God enlightens. And with me you shall teach the Torah to the children of Israel."

But Jethro the proselyte answered, "A candle stub can give light in the night, but can it enlighten beside the sun? You are the sun that enlightens Israel; let me bear the light of Israel into the night of the nations."

While Jethro the proselyte went among the nations spreading with the love of his heart the Torah of Moses, Zagzagel, in the school on high, taught the Torah to the angels; and in the Garden of Eden the Holy One, blessèd be he, taught it to the Righteous, who are above the angels.

And the Messiah, listening to the Torah, cried to the Holy One, "When shall my turn come, Lord? When shall I go down upon earth?"

And God answered him, "When all the peoples shall proclaim, 'We know, we practice the Torah of Moses, our master,' your turn shall have come; then, bearing in your heart, like David in his, the blood of Ruth the proselyte, you shall go down; and, as the waters of the sea fill the ocean, so the love of the Lord shall fill the whole earth."

CHAPTER XVI

THE WAY OF TRIALS

As the armies of the angels had circled about the throne of glory in the vision on Sinai, so Moses circled around the Tabernacle the tents of the Levites and of the twelve tribes in the camp in the wilderness.

Behind the throne of splendor he had seen the archangel Raphael with his armies and standard in the regions of the north and of darkness. North of the Tabernacle he placed the children of Merari who bear the beams and planks of the sanctuary and its pillars and sockets that are dark as night. North of the Merari, with a banner of onyx, beryl and jasper, he placed the tribes of Asher and Naphtali, obscured by sin, and Dan, blackened by idolatry.

Before the throne on high, Moses had seen the archangel Gabriel with his standard and armies in the regions of the south with its propitious dews and sustaining rains. To the south of the Tabernacle he placed the children of Kohath bearing the Ark from which shower the blessings of the Torah. To the south of Kohath, with a banner of sardonyx, emerald and topaz, he put the tribes of Gad and Simeon and Reuben, from which pours repentance.

Left of the throne was the archangel Uriel with his standard and armies in the regions of the west from where come hail and storms. To the west of the Tabernacle he put the children of Gershon who shelter in the service of the sanctuary. With a banner of agate, chrysolite and amethyst, he put the tribes of Benjamin, Manasseh and Ephraim, strong shields against stormy Amalek.

On the right of the throne was the archangel Michael with his standards and armies in the regions of the east from which comes the light. East of the Tabernacle God placed Aaron and Moses for from the Priest and the Prophet comes light upon Israel. East of Aaron and his sons and Moses, with the banner of ruby, garnet and sapphire, came Zebulun, resplendent in abundance, Issachar, radiant with knowledge, and Judah, illumined by his royalty.

Through Moses' virtue manna descended on the twelve regions of the camp from the twelve regions of the sky; through Miriam's virtue the twelve rivers welling from her spring divided the twelve camps in the desert into twelve gardens; through Aaron's virtue the cloud of glory above the Tabernacle raised over Israel twelve airy canopies with twelve jewels, shining on the breastplate of the High Priest—bright onyx, beryl, jasper, sardonyx, emerald, topaz, agate, chrysolite, amethyst, ruby, garnet and sapphire.

Now in the second year after leaving Egypt, on the 20th day of the second month, the time came when God wanted the Israelites to leave the Sinai wilderness for the Land of Promise. The cloud of glory, giving the signal in the heights, began to move. Instantly Moses commanded the trumpets to be blown. The twelve tribes folded up their tents and gathered together their flocks while Aaron and his sons took off the veil of the Holy of Holies to cover with it the holy Ark. They enveloped with blue the candlestick and the table and the altar of gold. Then the sons of Gershon took off the cloth of the Tabernacle, its standard and its entrance curtain and all the belongings of its court with the ropes and other gear. The sons of Merari took up the beams, traverses, pillars and joists with their cords and their gear. The treasures divided from the holy dwelling were placed on six chariots of brass drawn by the twelve immortal oxen.

The sons of Kohath had to take hold with their hands of the handles of the Ark they were to carry, but they dared not

approach it. Knowing that the two Cherubim hurl invisible lightning on those whose heart is not purified, they feared the death of
Nadab and Abihu. When they had taken courage and put their
shoulders beneath the heavy burden, they could not lift it. The
Ark weighed on them more heavily than all the mountains of the
world.

Then Moses cried, "Rise up, Lord; let your enemies be scattered
and let those who hate you flee before you."

Instantly the Ark, rising up, bore its bearers. Their feet, naked
above the ground, walked on air. Thus the children of Israel went
toward the Promised Land. The cloud of glory that covered their
heads came down to guide their steps on the way, filling up the
valleys and leveling the heights. To escort them, Miriam's twelve
rivers glided through the desert like twelve gigantic liquid serpents.

The twelve princes of the tribes bore a coffin by the side of the
Ark. How could such a thing be possible, ask our rabbis? So holy
was the Ark that its bearers, in order not to turn their backs on
the divine presence, walked backwards. Was it not defiling this holiness to join it to a coffin? No, for in the Ark went the Torah
and in the coffin Joseph, who had walked according to the Torah.

From Judah to Gad the nine tribes which went before the Ark
hurried on their way to put a distance between themselves and it.
From Ephraim to Dan the three tribes that followed it lagged
behind to avoid coming up with it. For like the schoolboy who,
when his lesson is finished, runs away quickly fearing to be recalled by his master, or returns slowly wishing to delay the new
lesson, the Israelites already fled the Torah in their hearts.

After three days the cloud rested, but while the tribes made
ready to set up their tents and the Levites to raise up the Tabernacle, the Ark, bearing its bearers whose feet walked in the air, did
not stop going forward. Then Moses said, "Return, O Lord, unto
the many thousands of Israel." Then the feet of its bearers came to
rest on the ground and the Ark, in its turn, came to rest there.

They had scarcely finished setting up their camp when the murmuring began again, "Then we have not yet arrived? How many years more shall we need? Where, then, is this Land of Promise flowing with milk and honey? Can we even be certain that it exists? How good the cucumbers of Egypt were and the melons and the onions and the meat, the meat of the flesh-pots! What have we received in exchange? Manna in the morning, manna in the evening, manna on the Sabbath, manna week in and week out!"

"Why do you complain?" Caleb or Joshua would ask. "It is the food of the angels."

But Abiram the scoffer replied, "Are we angels? Is what is good for the health of angels good for the health of people? Have you ever seen corn put into a mill to be ground and nothing come out below? We swallow your manna by our mouths and it remains entirely in our bellies. Supposing our bellies were to burst? Every body produces excrement. Are we alone in the world not to?"

And all cried, "Meat, meat! Certainly God can give it to us, since he is in the midst of us."

But why, Rabbi Simeon ben Johai asks, did they clamor so for meat? Had they not with them their sheep and their oxen whose flesh they could eat after offering it to God? And did not the manna itself take in their mouths all the flavors that their hearts could wish? Yes, indeed. But it did not take the flavors of forbidden meats and it was the flavors of forbidden meats that, in despite of the Torah, they wanted to eat.

And why, asks Rabbi Tanhuma bar Rabbi Hanalai, did the Holy One, blessèd be he, allow to all nations all foods and to Israel alone forbid almost all? It is like the doctor who had two patients—one was lost beyond hope, the other might recover. What did the doctor do? To the parents of the one who was to die he said, "Give him whatever he likes to eat." To the parents of the one whom he hoped to save, "Give him this, do not give him that." In the same way every nation must perish some day, why thus deprive it of what pleases it? But the children of Israel, if they deny themselves for the Torah's sake, will live to the last day.

When he heard the complaints of the Israelites, Moses complained to God, "Why have you afflicted your servant? Why have I not found favor in your sight and why do you lay the burden of this people on me? From where should I find flesh to give to them?"

"Go, say to them," answered the Lord, " 'You shall have so much meat you shall vomit it from the throat and the nostrils.' "

The Prophet, seeing God would not appease the Israelites except to punish them, pled with him, saying, "Why give way to them, Lord, and punish them afterward? Does a person say to an ox, 'Here are your oats, if you take them, I shall behead you'? Let me rather plead with them." And he sought the Israelites saying, "God has given you manna that is the food of the angels. Do you think that he cannot give you meat, the food of beasts? He will grant your wish, but if he grants it, you shall perish."

The best of them renounced their desire and withdrew beneath their tents, but the others cried out, "God no longer hears you. No longer does he grant your desire. It is to you that he refuses what we ask of him. You have sworn that he could do all things for us and you have no more power over him."

Then a wind blew whose tempest was so great that it could have destroyed the world. Quails fell as thick as snowflakes, concealing the eye of the sun and filling with night all the light between earth and heaven. On the north and the south of the camp, throughout an extent that would have needed seven days to cover, they stopped two cubits from the ground, so the sinner did not need to bend down to take them. But all those that tasted of them died. Thus this place was named Kibroth-Hattaavah, "The Groves of Lust." And Moses thought in his heart, "If it takes such reprimands to teach them to nourish their bodies, what rebukes must there be to teach them to nourish their souls?"

He continued to teach them the Torah while the judges judged them. Often, not knowing how to judge, the judges consulted the Prophet, and sometimes the Prophet had to give a severe judgment. But Aaron the High Priest, not having to punish, spread throughout Israel the gentleness of his soul. Did two neighbors quarrel? He went to each one and said to him, "Your brother is sad. He strikes his breast and blames himself and groans, 'How have I been able to offend my brother?' " If a husband was about to put away his wife, he hurried to the wife saying, "For her who can keep the love of her spouse, the altar of itself lights up with joy." To the husband he said, "On him who sends away the companion of his youth, the altar of itself lets fall tears."

Thus Aaron, forestalling justice, made peace and Moses thought in his heart, "Happy my brother who does not have to punish."

One day the judges brought before him two lawbreakers. One was Zelophehad, son of Hepher of the tribe of Manasseh, who had been found cutting down a tree on the Sabbath. Now it is written in the Torah, *Whoever violates the Sabbath shall die.* Moses sought excuses for him in his heart, "Perhaps he did not know that it was the Sabbath." His companions suggested, "Perhaps he was cutting wood for the altar of burnt offerings." But he had cut the wood to cook his food and to show to all his contempt for the Sabbath. Moses asked himself, "Shall I bring death on this person?" The other was Jahir, son of Shelomith of the tribe of Dan, whom Dathan had divorced after she had conceived from the embrace of Maror, the Egyptian taskmaster. She had brought up her son as an Israelite, but the tribe of Dan had driven him out. Moses, judging according to the Law, had approved in his judgment the tribe of Dan. The rage of Jahir had been aroused against Moses and against God and he had blasphemed the name of the Lord. It is written in the Torah, *The blasphemer shall die.* Moses sought excuses for him in his heart, but is there any excuse for blasphemy? The Prophet asked himself, "Shall I bring death on this person?"

In each case he consulted the Holy One, blessèd be he, who answered him, "Assemble the people and let the sinners be stoned before the face of the multitude."

"Punish them yourself, Lord," Moses implored him, "as you yourself punished idolatry and lust, punish blasphemy and violating the Sabbath, but do not command me to punish." Thus the Prophet implored him and he was grievously troubled because for the first time he must decree death.

But God replied, "I have entrusted to you my Torah. What will become of it if its guardian does not dare to guard it? Do you wish that I take it back from the world and that, deprived of it through your fault, the world remain unperfected?"

So the two men were stoned. A clamor rose from the Israelites, "What have we done? Why have we accepted the Torah? It promised us joy, but it brings curses. Take back your Torah, Moses. Give it back to the Eternal, for it will kill us all. We desire a Torah to live, not to die."

Once more the Prophet groaned to God, "Lord, Lord, why have you laid the burden of this people on me? How can I bear it? Deliver me from my task, Lord or kill me."

God answered him, "How long, my son, will you doubt yourself? Whom I choose is always strong enough. But since your humility seeks helpers, summon the Elders and, without diminishing the spirit that I have put on you, I will put it upon them. They shall be the Sanhedrin around you to pronounce on life or death and to guide the judges and to guide Israel."

Then the Prophet assembled the Elders before the Tabernacle and laid his hands on them. Without losing anything of its force, his spirit descended on them, like a flame that lights up other flames and shines among them, keeping its own brilliance. But the flame of Moses shone more brightly than all and the Elders shone around him like 70 smaller flames.

Now when Moses summoned the Elders to the Tabernacle, two among them, Eldad and Medad, thinking themselves unworthy, dared not enter. As a reward for their humility, the Holy One, blessèd be he, made the voice of prophecy speak in their souls. And Eldad prophesied, "Moses, our master, shall die and Joshua, the son of Nun, his disciple, shall succeed him, accomplishing his promise." And Medad prophesied, "Israel shall die and Israel shall live again and shall lead all the earth to the Land of Promise."

At these words Gershom, Moses' son, who was neither among the judges, nor among the priests, nor among the Elders, ran to the Prophet, crying, "Moses, our master, will you suffer the Elders to prophesy? They say that you will die and that Israel will die!"

Joshua, son of Nun, also cried out, "Moses, Moses, our master, they say that the disciple and not the master will keep the promises of the master!"

Moses replied, "Joshua, my son, you are my disciple. Do you think that your master is envious of his disciple's glory?" To Gershom he replied, "Gershom, my son, you are not a prophet. Why should I silence my prophets? Would God that all the children of Israel were prophets!"

That evening, to celebrate the light of God that had come on the Elders, their wives lighted lights before their dwellings. Perceiving this, Zipporah, Moses' wife asked, "What are these lights?"

Miriam replied to her, "The spirit of God descended on the Elders and their wives rejoice at it."

"Why do they not rather weep," answered Zipporah, "at least if the Elders imitate Moses, their master, for since he has known the spirit of God he has known my flesh no more."

In truth when the Lord, wanting to speak to the Israelites in the lightning of Sinai had commanded Moses, "For two days let the Israelites keep apart from their wives," the Prophet thought, "If during two days they are to keep apart from their wives to hear God only once, ought not I to keep from mine always, I who hear him always?" And he never again held Zipporah in his arms.

Out of ten parts of gossip which have been portioned to the world, women, say our rabbis, have taken nine for themselves. Thus it is not surprising if prophetesses themselves are not exempt. As soon as Miriam heard Zipporah's confidence, she hurried to Aaron her brother and told him of it, adding, "I too have received revelations from God; yet I have not refused joy to my husband." Aaron said in his turn, "I also have received revelations from God yet I have not refused myself to my wife." And both together concluded, "Our ancestors also received revelations without denying the joys of the flesh. Does Moses think himself wiser than the Patriarchs? Does he wish to humiliate us and show that he is a saint? It is his pride that he is showing and his pride is a sin."

But God said to them, "Whom do you judge, you whom I judge? I have uncovered for Moses all that is on earth below, all that is in heaven above, all that is before, all that is after. I have set him above my angels; he has seen with his eyes my divine presence. What he has done, I have wanted. You slander the master by slandering the servant, but you shall know the punishment of slanderers."

Next day the children of Israel made ready to depart to go up to the borders of the Promised Land. The tribes were folding up their tents. The Levites were taking apart the Tabernacle. Already the sacred pieces were on the chariots, drawn by the immortal oxen and the Ark had lifted up its bearers and the cloud of glory was setting forth when Aaron and Miriam appeared before Moses. Lo! both were defiled with leprosy.

"My sister, my brother!" cried the Prophet, "for what has God punished you? What have you done to deserve his anger?"

"Pardon us, pardon us, Moses. Because you know Zipporah no more, because you are wholly near God, we said evil of you. Our thoughts have defiled the purity of yours and God has put upon us impurity and defilement. Heal us! save us! Against you we have sinned and you alone can take away our sin!"

Long was Moses silent. Troubled by heavy grief, he thought, "My brother is against me, too; my sister, too, is against me!" And he shut his eyelids to keep back his tears.

At last he reopened his eyes and slowly let them rest on Aaron. As soon as he had looked on him the leprosy fell from his body. Then he looked on Miriam, but the more he looked upon her the more the defilement of leprosy thickened on her flesh.

Aaron cried, "Will you cast our sister out of the camp? She who watched over you on the bank of the river in Egypt? Who sang with you the Song of the Divided Waters? Who taught to the women the Torah of the Lord? Shall we enter the Land of Promise and Miriam not be with us?"

What did the Prophet do then? If he had prayed long, some would have said, "There is no end to his prayer, while there is no end to his sister's suffering." Others would have said, "For his sister his prayers are long; for us they are short." This is why, according to our rabbis, the Prophet prayed for a moment only. Then he took his rod and traced a circle around himself on the ground and he said to God, "So long as you do not remove the leprosy from Miriam, my sister, I will not leave this circle!"

God answered him, "If a king or if her father had spat in her face, she would bear her shame for seven days. Since I, the King of Kings, the Father of Fathers, have spat in her face, she should bear it for at least twice seven days. For your sake, my son, I will remit to her half of it. For one week let her be put out of the camp. At the end of the week I will cleanse her."

In memory of the seven hours which Miriam waited on the bank of the river till Moses should be saved from the waters, the tribes of Israel with their tents and their flocks, the sons of Gershon and Merari with the Tabernacle and the chariots and the sons of Kohath with the sacred Ark and the cloud of glory itself with the twelve jewels of the twelve splendors, for seven days waited until Miriam should be saved from the leprosy and should be given back to the Israelites with her renewed cleanness the cleanness of the twelve rivers sprung from her well.

But while the cloud and the Ark and the Levites and the tribes and the chariots and the flocks and the twelve rivers of the twelve fragrances, went forward again through the wilderness, Moses, who walked between Miriam and Aaron, thought in his heart, "Lord, Lord, how shall I be able to lead this people, if I am slandered in the ears of this people by Aaron, my brother, who is its High Priest and by Miriam, my sister, who is its prophetess?"

CHAPTER XVII

THE FRUIT OF THE LAND

When they had come to the wilderness of Paran on the borders of the Promised Land, the Prophet said to them, "Look, the land is before you. Take possession of it, but realize that if the Lord takes it away from the Canaanites, the Amorites, the Perizzites, the Hittites, the Hivites and the Jebusites, it is not because of your virtues, but because of their sins, for they prostitute their flesh before the face of their idols on every verdant mountain and in the hollows of the valleys they give their firstborn to the flames. If God gives to you what he takes back from them, it is not for your sakes, but for the sakes of Abraham and of Isaac and of Jacob, your ancestors, who have found grace in his sight."

To what can this be compared? asks Rabbi Aha the Great. To that king who said to his friend, "Come with me, I will give you a present." The friend accompanied him, but died on the way. What did the king do? He said to the son of his friend, "Your father is dead, but my promise still lives. Receive for your father the present that I promised." In the same way, God said to the children of Israel, "The land that I promised to your ancestors, behold I give it to you!" For the word of the Lord lives for ever.

But Korah, Pharaoh's former treasurer, replied to Moses, "Do we know this land? Do we know whether it will suit us? Shall we risk its invasion before exploring it?"

The young pushing the old, the old pushing the young, all pell-mell cried out after Korah, "We will not be deceived again. Let us first know where we are going. Send scouts who shall inform us."

"Has not the Lord informed you," Moses retorted, "and said to you, 'I lead you into a land of wheat and barley, of grapes and figs, of pomegranates and olives, of milk and honey, into a land over which the Lord watches and which is continually beneath his eye'? Did you send spies into the wilderness when I brought you up out of the land of Egypt? Now that I bring you out of the wilderness, do you wish to confirm the testimony of God?"

"No, not his testimony, but yours, who testifies for him," replied Korah. "The greater the enterprise, the greater should be one's prudence. I am no dreamer, I am a practical person."

And the young pushing on the old and the old pushing on the young, all pell-mell cried after him, "Let us be prudent, let us be prudent! This is a practical matter."

Moses thus chose twelve men, one for each tribe and commanded them, "Go, explore the land. Do not go on the highroad, but neither go by hidden pathways like robbers. Worship not the idols, but neither say that you will come to overthrow them. Look on the land, if it is firm it is fat; if it is soft it is thin. Look on the towns, if they are open their inhabitants are strong; if they are shut within walls they are cowards. You shall enter by the south and go up the valley and come down by the plain."

Why, ask our rabbis, did he make them enter by the south? It is because in the south are the poorest places in Canaan and the poorest places in Canaan are richer than the richest in Egypt. Like the merchant who first shows his less beautiful fabrics in order afterwards to spread out ones more beautiful and then yet more beautiful, he wished to lead them from splendor to marvel, so that their return should make each and all marvel.

On the 22nd day of the month of Sivan they left Kadesh-Barnea which is in the wilderness of Paran: Shammua for the tribe of Reuben; Shaphat for the tribe of Simeon; Igal for Issachar; Palti,

Gaddiel and Gaddi for Benjamin, Zebulon and Manasseh; Ammiel, Geuel, Sethur, Nahbi for Dan, Gad, Asher and Naphtali.

Our doctors have said, "There are beautiful names borne by those whose actions are beautiful and beautiful names borne by those whose actions are ugly. There are ugly names borne by those whose actions are beautiful. But these bore names that were ugly and their actions were ugly for their names contained shadow, imposture, blasphemy and the spirit of evil. Without learning from the leprosy that had punished Miriam, their mouths slandered the gifts of the Lord. Only Caleb from Judah and Joshua from Ephraim were beautiful in their names and in their actions. Caleb means, *Like unto the heart* and he spoke according to his heart, and Joshua means, *Savior* and he saved Israel.

On the 22nd day of the month of Sivan they left and on the eighth day of the month of Ab they returned. But how, ask our sages, could they in 40 days journey through the whole extent of the land of Israel? It was because, in its joy at being tread by the children of Israel, the land, shortening its ways, ran to meet them!

How great was the joy in the camp when they returned! The first two bore on their shoulders two poles from which hung a huge bunch of grapes. Now when a man loads his own shoulders he can bear a weight of one seah; when another loads him he can bear two; think, then, of the weight of this bunch carried on two poles by two men that four men had loaded. All, seeing it, cried, "How good is the land that the Lord gives us!" But when the spies followed by the multitude had come before Moses, joy ceased.

Humans, say our masters, have six organs to serve them. Three serve as they wish, three serve as directed; their eyes do not choose to see, nor their ears to hear, nor their noses to smell; but their feet walk at their will, their hands take hold at their will and at their will their mouths utter lies or truths. Now these lied.

According to the custom of slanderers, Shaphat began by praising, "We came to the land where you sent us and it is certainly good to look upon. See the bunch of grapes that we have brought back. Olives, figs, pomegranates are in the same measure. Honey flows from the trees, fat from the fields, milk from the cows...."

"But ..." said Palti.

"But," said Gaddiel, "it is a land without a Nile. It must be watered and to water it there must be water from the sky."

"What shall we do if it does not rain?" asked Korah.

"We shall wait for the rain," said Abiram.

"Then," others said, "no more grapes, no more pomegranates, no more figs, no more olives, no more fat, no more milk, no more honey? And it is for this land that Egypt has been taken from us?"

"Then," continued Gaddi, "pestilence is everywhere."

"Pestilence?"

"It is a land that devours its inhabitants. In each city we entered we saw but burials."

"Pestilence? Pestilence? Pestilence on Moses!"

Then Joshua rose up and cried, "Believe them not. They lie because they are afraid."

"Yes," said Shammua, "we were afraid."

"Yes," said Gaddiel, "we were afraid. You also would have been afraid."

"Of whom?"

"Of the three sons of Anak: Ahiman, Sheshai, Talmai.... They are giants! They are descended from the angels who coupled with the daughters of men after the Flood. They only die by halves. When half their body is dead, the other half doubles itself and replaces it.... Their legs are higher than the mountains. Their arms are longer than the rivers; their heads rise to heaven.... All twelve of us were hidden in a cave and this cave was but a hole pierced by the sting of a bee in the skin of a pomegranate that their daughter was eating. And when she had eaten, she threw all twelve of us, with the cave, into the grass of her garden!"

"And," continued Gaddi, "the sons of Anak are but three, but there are also the sons of Amalek who are without number. Esau their ancestor, the enemy of old, has posted them on the frontier to bar our passage."

And all cried, "The sons of Amalek, the sons of Amalek!" for Amalek to the Israelites is like a whip to the child. When Amalek is spoken of they remember the whip. "God hates us, God hates us!" they howled. "He takes Egypt from us and gives us Amalek!"

"Have I not already led you against Amalek?" cried Joshua. "He ran before you as the wind over the plain."

"What! Joshua dare speak? Shut his mouth!... A man of war who wants war!... What are our sons to you? You have no sons.... With no sons he is not a man. With no sons he is an assassin."

Then Caleb rose up. Beside his voice, thunder was silence; the giants, when they had heard it, had fled. He cried, "Listen not to them. Terror is beneath their tongue. They lie!... I had to prick them with my sword to make them bring you this bunch of grapes. Listen to me! Listen to me! I went up to Machpelah into the cave where sleep the Patriarchs. Abraham, Isaac and Jacob rose up from their tomb. They told me that they await you. I swore to them that you would come. Are they not stronger than Amalek? Is not God stronger than the Patriarchs? To deliver to you the Canaanite, the Amorite, the Perizzite, the Hittite, the Hivite and the Jebusite he has cast out from their land their guardian angels. We were as grasshoppers before the giants; he made us in their eyes greater than giants. Speak to them, Moses, speak to them!"

But Moses was silent. Shrouded in sackcloth, with ashes on their heads, the ten slanderers went throughout the camp; they cried aloud, "Woe to our daughters who shall be defiled by Amalek! Woe to our sons who shall be butchered by Amalek! The towns that we saw have walls larger than the night; the men that we saw have in the foreheads two suns for eyes!"

The children of Israel howled after them, "Woe! Woe! Abiram, Dathan, become our chieftains! Lead us, lead us back into Egypt!" The young and the old pushing on each other pell-mell, they surrounded Moses, Aaron, Caleb and Joshua. Gathering stones, they stoned them, and like hailstones the stones fell on them.

Seeing the redness of blood on the foreheads of the righteous, the cloud of glory descended from above the Tabernacle and came down to cloak them in a mantle of onyx, beryl, jasper, sardonyx, emerald, topaz, chrysolite, amethyst, ruby, garnet and sapphire; but the Israelites howled on and, stoning the cloud, stoned God.

All night beneath the roof-skins of their tents, crouching in the dust, grinding their teeth, clawing their cheeks, tearing out their beards, hammering the ground with their foreheads, the 60 myriads of Israel wailed, and the trembling of their terror tore heaven with the 600,000 rendings of their cry.

Then God said to them, "You weep without reason. I will give you two reasons for weeping." On that ninth night of the month of Ab the Lord decreed the overthrow of the Temple and the scattering of their posterity from the land that they had not wanted. That same night of Ab 2,000 years later he overthrew the Temple and scattered them. And 2,000 years after, on that same night of Ab, scattered over the earth, Israel still weeps.

Then the Holy One, blessèd be he, said to the Prophet, "You are silent, my son? You do not plead for them?"

"Not for them, Lord, but for you! If you abandon them now, what will the nations say? That you have not been able to keep your people; that your people have not wished to keep you; that against the gods of Egypt you were strong enough, but against those of Canaan your arm is too short; that in the desert you were able to lead them; that into the Land of Promise you were not able. If you destroy them, what will the worlds say? They will say, 'Does this God know anything except destruction? He has de-

stroyed the generation of the Flood; he has destroyed the generation of Babel; he has destroyed the generation of Sodom; he has
destroyed the Egyptian; and now he destroys the children of Israel!' For ages to come you shall be a God of hate, O you God of
Love! I am nothing; your children of Israel are nothing. They have
in no way deserved your forgiveness; yet pardon them, if not for
them, for me or if not for me, for yourself, King of the World."

When he had spoken, without any word, amid the howlings of
the night, God answered him.

Next day, in the morning, Moses assembled the tribes and said
to them, "When will you understand the Eternal? For you he
divided the sea; scarcely had you passed dryshod than you asked
once more for the bondage of Egypt. For you he rained down
manna; scarcely had you tasted it than you demanded to have your
excrement. He gave himself to you on Sinai, you worshiped the
Golden Calf. For you he gave me his Torah, you begged him,
'Take back your Torah.' Now that he brings you to the Promised
Land, you cry to him, 'Take back your land and your promise.'

"Do you think he needs to destroy you, armies, giants or
Amalekites? He who with a word made the world, with a word
can destroy it.

"Nevertheless, you shall not all perish; for thus says the Lord,
'The ten slanderers shall be punished according to their crime;
their tongues shall come forth out of their mouths and, covered
with vermin, shall descend unto their navels and they shall die in
the vermin of their slander. Joshua and Caleb shall have, as their
reward in the Land of Promise, the portions of those who slandered it. As for you who have refused it, you shall have no part
in it. Your wives shall enter it, for they have not sinned, neither
on the shore of the sea, nor at the feet of the idol, nor concerning
Torah, nor the manna, nor by slander. But not one of those who
were numbered at the going out from Egypt and who today are of

20 years and upward, shall see the Land of the Eternal. Each year before the ninth night of the month of Ab they shall count themselves and each year on that night a fortieth part of their number shall die in the wilderness. Their bones shall rot in the wilderness, for by refusing the land of life they have refused life itself; but I will teach their children and make of them a new generation that has not known Egypt nor the idols of Egypt nor its sins, nor your sins. That generation shall possess the land that the Torah has promised.' "

Then they knew their sin and now, in their repentance, they groaned in shame, as before they had groaned in fear, "What have we done, what folly was ours? Has not God loaded us with miracles? Why should he refuse them to us today? No, we will not wander 40 years in the wilderness. We will follow the Lord to the land that he gives us. When he sees our contrite hearts he will give it to us. To arms! Let us go up the mountain! Let us fall upon Amalek. The Lord will be with us, if we are with him."

In vain Moses tried to hold them back. He said to them, "It is too soon. Your souls are not yet ripe for the vintage of the Lord."

But at once resuming their impudence, they answered, "Stay behind! We will conquer without you. Do you think God needs you to do his miracles?"

Arming in haste, pell-mell, the young pushing on the old, the old pushing on the young, without consulting the twelve jewels of the High Priest, without bearing into the battle the holy Ark, they threw themselves on Amalek, who waited for them in the narrow passes. Their blood flowed like the torrents of the mountain. Moses led back their disorder to Hormah. But he brought back also the grapes of Canaan and so abundant was the wine of those grapes that there is enough, until the end of the world to fill, each Sabbath, the cup that the Lord blesses.

CHAPTER XVIII

THE REBELLION OF KORAH

Israel camped in the wasteland of Kadesh-Barnea. To bring up the new generation, Moses taught the Torah to the children for, say our teachers, the world rests upon the breath of the children who learn the Torah.

When a year had passed, on the eighth day of the month of Ab, the trumpet was sounded in the camp and the crier cried, "Dig yourselves graves!" The 600,000 Israelites dug 600,000 graves in the sand. They lay down in them and all night from the open graves their groans rose to heaven. Next day at dawn the crier cried, "Let the living get up from the dead." Those who still lived rose up; 15,000 old men remained stretched in the dust.

Then murmuring broke out anew. Dathan the slanderer said to the survivors, "Will you give 15,000 corpses to Moses each year? Is it not better to risk our courage once for all against the Canaanite and the Amorite, the Hittite and the Jebusite?"

"No," replied Abiram the scoffer, "they prefer certain death to doubtful victory."

"Do you not see," continued Dathan, "that Moses decimates you in order the better to reign over you? Why exhaust yourselves in the desert for 40 years by ceaseless marches, only to die?"

"They are fond of walking," Abiram the scoffer retorted, "and they prefer moving over well-warmed sand to the idleness of repose beneath the shade of the fig tree."

For a long time Korah, Pharaoh's former treasurer who had brought from Egypt all the treasures of Joseph, had resented the power of the Prophet. He said, "Why is Moses our chief? I am richer than he." His wife Olla, like him, proud, inflamed his pride yet further. It is of her doubtless that it is written, *A foolish woman plucks down her house with her own hands.* For what good did Korah get of his riches? A bad wife is the ruin of her husband and without a good wife no treasure is truly a treasure.

When he came home in the evening, Olla asked him, "What has your master Moses taught today?"

"He has taught the *zizith.*"

"And what are the *zizith?*"

"They are fringes of blue-purple which we must put on the four corners of the *tallith* to remember the Sabbath."

"And what is a *tallith?*"

"It is the praying-shawl."

"If I make you a *tallith* wholly of blue-purple will you still need, to remember the Sabbath, blue fringes at the four corners? Ask Moses, your master. And what more did he teach you?"

"The *mezuza.*"

"What is the *mezuza?*"

"A small box containing 22 lines from the Torah which we must nail up to the doorpost to remind us of the Lord."

"If you have in your house the whole Torah, must you still have, to remind you of the Lord, the 22 lines of the *mezuza?* Ask Moses your master."

Korah went to find Moses and asked him while he was teaching the Torah to the children, "Moses, our master, if my *tallith* is wholly of blue-purple, shall I still need the *zizith?* If I have in my house the whole Torah, shall I still need the *mezuza?*"

"Let your ear hear what your mouth utters," Moses answered; "you must still have the *zizith,* you must still have a *mezuza.*"

"Then," retorted Korah, "four fringes in blue-purple are more powerful than a whole *tallith* of blue-purple; 22 lines of the Torah are more powerful than the whole Torah?"

And he went about saying, "The Torah is absurd. Can absurdity come from God? It is Moses who invented it to oppress us."

Moses thought, "How shall I be able to make the new generation, if the old generation undoes the Law?"

One evening Korah came home with his head shaven. No one on the way had recognized him. "Who has disfigured you?" cried his wife.

"Moses," he answered; "but he dressed his brother Aaron like a bride to lead him to the Tabernacle."

"He has humiliated you."

"Yet he also shaved his two sons and all the Levites in the same way."

"What do the others matter to him, as long as he humiliates you? He envies your riches; he hates you and you permit him to do anything! Is it right that Elizaphan, your cousin, is the chief of the descendants of Kohath who bear the Ark? Your grandfather Kohath had four sons—Amram, Izhar, Hebron and Uzziel. The two sons of Amram, Moses and Aaron, are High Priest and Prophet, which is a lot. Ought not you, the oldest of the second, Izhar, come before a son of the youngest son of your grandfather? You have let Elizaphan be put in your place. How long shall Moses laugh at us? Who has made him king that you should obey him? Free yourself. I desire a husband who commands."

Then Korah resolved to destroy Moses and the work of Moses.

First of all he assembled the poor and said to them, "Have you considered what Moses will cost you, with Aaron his High Priest and his prohibitions and his ordinances and his tithes? Suppose I had for my neighbor a widow, the mother of two daughters, who had but one field. She came to plow it, but Moses said to her, *You shall not plow with an ox and an ass together.* The Lord forbids it! She went to sow, but Moses said to her, *You shall not sow with unlike seeds.* The Lord forbids it! She came to harvest and to bind the sheaves. Moses said to her, *Leave the gleanings for the poor and for the poor leave the sheaves in the corners of the field.* The Lord commands it! She went to store the grain in the barn; he said to her, *You shall give me the first and second tithe.* The Lord commands it! Then what did she do? She sold her field and bought two sheep in order to clothe herself with their fleeces and profit by their yield. When they had lambs, Aaron came and said to her, 'Give me the firstborn, for thus the Holy One, blessèd be he, has prescribed.' She gave up her firstborn. Came the time of shearing, Aaron said to her, 'Give me the first fleece, for thus has commanded the Holy One, blessèd be he.' When she had given it to him, she thought, 'It is not in my power to resist this man. Thus I will kill my sheep and I will eat them.' When they were slain, Aaron said to her, 'Give me the shoulders, the jaws, the stomach, for it is the law of God.' And she cried out, 'What! Even when they are slain I cannot save them from your hand? Then let them be cursed!' But he answered, 'Then they belong to me wholly, for thus has decreed the Holy One, blessèd be he.' And he took them and went. The widow remained weeping and her two daughters with her."

Thus Korah scoffed at the Torah before the multitude. Then he added, "You will all weep like that widow if you continue to let Moses and Aaron lead you."

Some applauded, others remained silent. But if Medad, Eldad, Caleb, Phinehas or Joshua came by, reminding them of the Prophet's virtues, and proclaimed, "If he should order us to take a ladder to climb to heaven, we ought to do it!" Korah was forgotten.

Then he turned to the princes of the tribes, "The people groan beneath the yoke of Moses, but they know not what else to do except to groan and cry out. Will you also be content with tears and clamor? Moses has made himself king; he has made his brother Aaron High Priest, his nephews Eleazar and Ithamar chiefs of the priests. He has given the instruction of the women to his sister Miriam; to his sister's husband Caleb the portion of the spies; to his sister's grandson Bezalel the building of the Tabernacle; to the son of his nephew Phinehas the guarding of the entrance of the Tabernacle; and to his favorite disciple Joshua the command of the army. I ask not for myself; I am descended from Levi, but is it just that the tribe of Levi should be set above all? Why should it receive a tithe from the others? Why is the High Priest a Levite? Would not a prince of Judah, Benjamin, Ephraim, Manasseh, Reuben or of Simeon be as good a High Priest as Aaron?"

Having heard him, the princes of the tribes appeared before Moses and said, "Why is the tribe of Levi set above all? Why does it receive the tithe from the others? Why is the High Priest a Levite? Why should not one of us be High Priest?"

Moses answered them, "The Lord has set the bounds to the world he has created. He has divided light from darkness, Israel from the nations, Levi from Israel. For neither families nor races nor things are alike in his creation. Each has its place, each its function. Let the peoples inhabit the earth, let Israel enlighten the peoples and let Levi enlighten Israel as the sun lights the heavens, for it would be easier to make alike day and night than to make alike the peoples and Israel, and Israel and Levi. But if you doubt that it is so by God's command, let each of you take a rod of dry wood and on it write his name for his tribe; Aaron also will take his rod and mark on it his name for the tribe of Levi. We will lay all these rods in the Tabernacle and await the choice of the Lord."

They did it and on the morrow, when they came to take their rods, they saw that the rod of Aaron had flowered and had brought forth an almond blossom.

But Abiram cried, "It had more sap than the others; it has merely put forth again," and none bowed before the Lord's choice.

Meanwhile Korah, who knew in advance that God would choose Levi, went everywhere repeating, "If the High Priest must be a son of Levi, why must this son of Levi be Aaron?" He gathered around him, together with the chiefs of the tribes, the chief among the Levites, the powerful and the rich, and Dathan the slanderer and Abiram the scoffer and their friends, all the scoffers and slanderers; and having in mockery dressed them in the *tallith* blue-purple, he gave them, some 250, a feast. When they were full of meat, he said, "To free ourselves from Moses let us first of all cast down Aaron. Since the tribe of Levi is chosen to be the first, let a Levite be a High Priest first; then we will each be priest in our turn and each in turn will make his Torah." He thought in his heart, "It is I who will be High Priest and when I am High Priest, High Priest I will remain and my Torah will be the Torah."

But, ask our Elders, from where did his assurance come? Korah was crafty and experienced, distinguishing the possible from the impossible. By what blindness did he rush to his doom? But having been a bearer of the Ark, he had seen the future and, seeing the future, he had perceived, issuing from himself, a whole line of prophets coming right down to the prophet Samuel. He did not imagine that his sons and his grandsons would do penance for his faults and through their penance deserve their exaltation. Seeing no prophets among the seed of Moses, he said to himself, "Certainly God wants me, who shall be the father of so many prophets, to pass before Aaron the High Priest and before Moses the Prophet."

At the end of the feast, Eleazar and Ithamar, Aaron's sons, came to claim the portion for the Tabernacle. But the banqueters chased them away, crying, "We recognize Aaron as High Priest no longer; we recognize Moses no longer as Prophet!"

They went to complain to Moses, who said to them, "Their feasting has clouded their understanding; when the night is passed, then will light return."

Next day Moses summoned Abiram and Dathan to the tribune of the Torah, for the Law does not permit an evildoer to be condemned without being heard. But they answered him, "We will not go up!" The madman unknowingly prophesied his own doom. Truly they did not go up, but went down to the flames of hell.

Having heard their refusal, the Prophet himself went to the doors of their tents, thinking, "Then I shall have done all that I can; let them, for the last time, have a chance to repent."

They would not let him enter, barring the threshold by their loud sarcasm and insult. "What do you bring us, son of Amram," cried Abiram the scoffer, "locusts or lice? Hail or darkness?"

"And what do you come to take from us?" cried Dathan the slanderer. "If it is our gold, you have already taken it for your Tabernacle. If it is our cattle, you have already taken them for your offerings. If it is our daughters, they have passed their eighth year—too old for your pleasures!"

Moses thought, "Woe to them that weary the patience of God!" And he left them.

The envy that incites rebellion is sinful, say our teachers. In order that peace may reign in the heavens, the Lord permits not that the moon shall look upon the stars that shine above her, nor that the stars shall look on the sun, that is more resplendent than they.

Sinful, say our sages, is rebellion that engenders envy, for what shall become of the vessel that has lost its pilot, what shall become of the people that has lost its guide?

As he returned to the Tabernacle, Moses saw the multitude in uproar, listening to the words of Korah and the Levites and the princes allied with him. The applause changed to hooting at his approach, acclamation to jeers. The anger of the people, bellowing from 600,000 voices like the fires of the mountain of old, mimicked the anger of God. The Prophet said to Korah, "What do you want? The crown of the High Priest. Did Aaron take it? Was it I that gave it to him? If I had been able to choose, would I not have crowned my son or myself, rather than load my own head with your hatred, yet without setting upon it the glory that you covet? You are 250 men; can there be 250 High Priests? We have but one

Torah, we have but one God and God has set Aaron his High Priest before the Ark in the Holy of Holies where he has set his Torah. If it please a king to set his slave on his throne, is not to rebel against the slave to rebel against the king? The Lord has chosen his servant. Who battles the servant, battles the Lord."

"Are you," replied Koran, "the only one to know the will of God? You pretend that he speaks to you secretly when none can hear his voice nor see his face. But has he not spoken to us all before the eyes of the whole world? Were you alone on Sinai when his Ten Words were sounded? Were you alone when his face appeared in the midst of the flame and the thunder? We have all seen him, we have all heard him. Why should you alone speak in his name? Does Abraham's blessing rest on you alone? Are we not all children of Israel? Children old enough to choose a leader or not to choose one if we do not desire one?"

"Yes, yes," cried the multitude; "we are all equal! We no longer want a leader. You, our leader, have flouted the Ten Words of Sinai that we all heard. You have stolen from us the joys of Egypt, the fleshpots, the sure bread.... You lied to us about your Land of Promise that exists nowhere, that we shall never see.... You wanted to become all-powerful through our slavery.... You have dishonored by your cursing Israel that is your father and mother!... You have committed adultery with the souls of our wives!... By taking away all rest from our days and our nights, you have broken the Sabbath rest. You have killed us by hunger and thirst and pestilence in the desert and you wanted to kill us, through 40 years, by repentance!... You have profaned the name of the Lord by forcing it to work miracles against us.... You have made an idol of flesh by making of yourself an idol.... And you have blasphemed the One God for you said, 'I am Moses, your God.' "

He answered them, "Fools! I was king in Egypt and for you I left my royal estate. I was shepherd in Midian and for you I left my solitude. I spoke before Pharaoh; I divided the sea; I fed you with miracles as a mother feeds her child with milk. For 40 days and 40 nights I fasted on the mountain to meditate on the Law of your salvation. I shattered this Law to take on myself the burden of your sins. I faced death 40 times beneath the stones hurled by your hands and 40 times I have begged God to pardon you! He has pardoned your cries of suffering and your cries of anger, for the Lord is just and long-suffering. When someone cries out in anger or pain, does he give no ear?

"May he pardon you today once more, for you cry out in ignorance. Others have put your complaints into your mouths. Them the Lord shall not pardon for they cry not out in anger, in pain or in ignorance. Their cry is envy and they know what they say. These proud, the scoffers, the slanderers, the rich, the princes of the tribes and the princes of the Levites, understand, see, and should enlighten you. They extinguish the light, they tear up the Torah in the night, they throw the world back into the chaos of the night. Keep apart from them. Depart far from the tents where they dwell. On them is hurled the anathema; I cast them out from Israel and from the Lord."

While the multitude drew back in silence and terror, he cried to Korah, the princes, the Levites and the 250 sinners on whom his cursing fell, "Tomorrow come to the Tabernacle. Each of you bring a censer and put fire in it and incense. You shall all, with Aaron, offer your incense before the Lord. I shall not be there, but God will be there. Once again he shall show his servant. You yourselves shall do the miracle that shall open the eyes of Israel."

In the night the Lord said to the Prophet, "Moses, my son, what do you want me to do?"

"Have you created hell, King of the World?" replied Moses. "If you have created it, engulf them."

"What!" answered the Lord, "you who were wont to demand pardon, now you demand punishment? You, who would pardon them when they rebelled only against me, now, because they rebel against you, would no longer pardon them? I told you, 'When my face is justice, yours shall be mercy,' and now when my face is mercy, yours is justice."

"How, Lord, shall I make a new generation if the old continue and if it destroy it in advance?"

"In 40 years they will all die."

"The rebels must die today or your Torah will be dead before it has lived."

As God remained silent, the sun and the moon appeared before him, crying, "Lord, the sinners that Moses condemns, our eyes will no longer see them. If you do not cast them out, we will light the world no more."

"Rebel lights! You lit the generations of the Deluge and Babel and Sodom that I had condemned and now you would not light those whom a mortal condemns?" And to constrain them to their tasks, he hurled on them his lightnings. Since that day, says Rabba, at every dawn and at every evening God himself has to hurl the moon and the sun into the day and the night for they refuse to light sinners.

Moses still implored him, crying, "Lord, Lord, was it I who asked you to be their leader? Have I not pled with you to leave me in my obscurity? I have followed and served you. For you I have suffered reproaches and anguish. What shall become of me, what shall I do if your enemies triumph? Have you not sworn to me your help? Do not abandon me. Be the director of my work, or if these die in their beds the common death of all and you do not light against them the fires of your wrath, I consent to cry out that you are not God and that Moses is not your servant."

Then God said, "When a saint commands, God obeys."

On, the son of Peleth, had a virtuous wife, Dinah. It is of her doubtless that it is written, *Every wise woman builds her house, for the price of a virtuous woman is far above rubies. Her children rise up to call her blessed and her husband also praises her.* Dinah, when she heard of the Prophet's anathema, counseled her husband, "Do not go tomorrow to the Tabernacle for the offering of incense. What difference will it make? If Moses carries the day, you will be a follower of Moses. If Korah carries the day, you will be a follower of Korah."

He answered, "Moses is great; I repent me. But I have given my oath to Korah; I cannot go back on my oath."

What did Dinah do? She made him drunk with strong liquor and on the morrow he did not wake. While he was yet asleep, lo! his bed began to shake, flames and smoke came up from the earth. The bed trembled and the earth opened. Dinah seized hold of her husband who was already choking in the gulf and she cried out, "God of justice, will you punish repentance?" Thus was On, the son of Peleth, saved.

At the same moment the thundering jaws of the abyss opened to devour with fiery teeth Abiram and Dathan and all their friends and all their children, even to the newborn; for so baleful is rebellion, say our elders, that it destroys the innocent with the guilty. Korah, the princes of the tribes, the princes of the Levites and all their confederates, had raised up simultaneously with Aaron, their censers before the Holy of Holies. From the eyes of the Cherubim there sprang 500 lightnings; without a sound or a cry these entered into the nostrils of the wicked and extinguished their souls within their unscathed bodies. While the Wrath stretched upon the ground 250 corpses, Aaron, alone upright, lifted up his hand to God in the incense rising from his censer. Beneath Korah's corpse the ground disappeared; burned already by the fire from on high, he was burned again by the fires of hell.

Thus Abiram the scoffer, Dathan the slanderer and Korah the proud perished; for, say our sages, the presence of God rests neither on the proud, the slanderer or the scoffer. It rests on the meek.

Rabba bar Hana recounts how one day, as he was journeying through the desert, an Arab came up to him and said, "Come, I will show you the place where Korah was swallowed up."

He took a rag of wool, dipped it in water and rolled it round the point of his lance, then struck the ground with it. Smoke came up and in the smoke a voice cried, "We lied! We lied! It is the God of Moses that is God, the Torah of Moses that is the Torah."

When the sinners had perished, Moses said, "Now let me make the generation of the Torah."

CHAPTER XIX

THE INSTRUCTION IN THE WILDERNESS

For 40 years they wandered in the wilderness, going from Kadesh to Rithmah, from Libnah to Rissah, from Shepher to Haradah. Miriam's twelve rivers followed them to quench their thirst; Aaron's cloud hovered above their heads and went before them—burning up thorns and serpents and tigers, filling up the valleys, leveling mountains, blinding with terror the peoples; and the manna of Moses refreshed their flesh with the purity of its changing flavors.

Every year on the ninth day of the month of Ab 15,000 old men remained stricken in the open graves and the survivors recounted to them who had been born in the desert the bondage in Egypt, the ten plagues on Pharaoh, the sea divided for the tribes set free, the fiery law given on the mountain, the Golden Calf, the rebellion, the land that was offered and the God that was refused. They said, "Happy you who shall inhabit the land where dwells the Holy One! Of it we have seen but one bunch of grapes. We shall die without touching the vine on which they grew. Taste not of our sins; gather the fruit of our repentance." But many thought in their hearts, "Have we not suffered enough? Why should we perish without reward? Why should these who come after us have more than we? Shall others possess that which was promised to us? Let them sin in their turn so that they perish like us."

But all honored Moses, who was now bringing up the new generation.

Why, ask our rabbis, was the Torah taught in the wilderness? Because before the Torah the world was but a wilderness and because without the Torah it would become a wilderness again.

Every night, in the middle of the night, Joshua, son of Nun, the disciple among the disciples, prepared the linen shirt on the pillow of his still sleeping master and shook the dust from his miter, his tunic and his sandals and placed them near the bed. He went to draw water for cleansing, and in the court of waving walls he arranged the seats in their semicircles and the raised throne. Then he commanded the crier to cry, "Assemble to hear the word of God!" And while the disciple served the master and dressed him, the children and the youth and the men went to the princes of the tribes, to the Elders, to Eleazar and Aaron, who led them in procession to the feet of the Prophet to wish him the joy of the morning. Then all escorted him to the Tabernacle where Joshua seated him on the golden throne. Then, taking up the lesson at the place where on the previous day he had left it, Moses would speak.

Great is peace, our elders have said, for between the angels of snow and the angels of fire the Lord in Heaven has set peace. If the angels themselves have need of peace on high, how much more does humankind need it here below?

Great is peace, our doctors have said, for in order that it exist, the Eternal permits the divine name itself to be blotted out.

Great is peace, our sages have said, for war itself begins by a summons to peace.

This is why the Prophet taught, "When you go out to fight, say to the people, 'If a person has built a house and has not yet dedicated it, let him return to his house, for he may fall in the battle and another dedicate it. If someone has planted a vine and has not yet enjoyed its fruit, let him return to his vine, for he may die in battle and another shall have this pleasure. If someone is engaged and has not yet married, let him return to his wife, for he may die in the battle and another marry her. If any have fear in their hearts, let them return, lest this fear be contagious. Thus shall peace dwell among you. Before beginning battle, say to the enemy, 'Let peace be made between us.' If he refuse it, only then shall you take your weapons."

Bukki, son of Jogli, asked, "Moses, our master, you have taught, *Great is peace.* Why, then, must there be war?"

And Moses answered, "To make a greater peace."

He taught again, "When you have entered the land that God gives you, you shall divide it among you, family by family; each shall have its field and its vine and none shall have more than another. Six years you shall sow your fields, six years you shall harvest your vines and they shall give their fruit. But the seventh year shall be a Sabbath of rest unto the land, a Sabbath for the Lord. In that year you shall not sow your field nor prune your vine. They shall belong to all—to you and to your servant, your maidservant, your hired servant and the foreigner sojourning with you and to your cattle and the beasts that are in the land. Then you shall number seven times seven years and you shall cause the trumpet of the Jubilee to sound on the tenth day of the seventh month. On the Day of Atonement shall you make the trumpet sound throughout all your land. You shall hallow the 50th year and proclaim liberty throughout all the land to all the inhabitants therein. It shall be a Jubilee for you and you shall return to everyone their possessions. You shall return all slaves to their families, for God will not tolerate that any who have heard the Word of the Lord be enslaved nor will God allow that field be added to field and vine to vine, for 'the land is mine,' says the Lord."

Kemuel, son of Shaphtan, asked, "Moses, our master, you say, 'The earth is the Lord's and the fullness thereof.' Why then must Israel have its portion of earth?"

Moses answered, "So that one day it may give back to God the whole extent of earth."

The Prophet said again, *Hear, O Israel, the Lord is our God, the Lord is One,* you shall love the Lord your God with all your heart and with all your soul and with all your might, and you shall love your neighbor as yourself. For God created humankind in his own image. To love another is to love God. Thus when the Lord shall have cast out from before you the peoples whom he dispossesses, keep yourself from walking in their ways. Do not ask after their gods, saying, How did these nations serve their gods so I can do likewise. You shall not do so unto the Lord your God, for every abomination unto the Lord, which he hates, have they done unto their gods, for they have even burned their sons and daughters in the fire to their gods. Thus in the Lord's land practice the Torah in purity and in love. For if you do not stray from his command-ments, neither to the right nor to the left, you shall be blessèd in your city and blessèd in your field. Blessèd shall be the fruit of your loins and blessèd the fruit of your soil. Blessèd shall be your baskets and your pans. Blessèd shall be your birth and your death, blessèd your life after your death. The Lord, as he has sworn, will make of you a nation of priests who shall unite the peoples one with another and shall unite them to God. If you do not observe in your land the Covenant that the Lord your God has made with your ancestors, you shall be tormented in your city and plagued in your field, vexed shall be the fruit of your loins and plagued the fruit of your soil; afflicted your pans and your baskets; tormented your birth and your death; and cursed your life after your death. The sky above your head shall be of brass and the earth beneath your feet shall be of iron. The Lord shall strike you with dizziness and blindness and you shall go groping through the light like the blind through night. Because you do not serve the Lord your God with joy in the time of abundance, you shall serve your enemies in hunger, thirst and wretchedness. The Lord shall scatter you among the peoples throughout all the earth and shall make you a reproach to the peoples. He will put anguish into your heart and trembling into your flesh. In the morning you shall say in terror, 'Would it were still night,' and at evening, 'Would it were still morning,' and you shall scarcely know if you still live. For God desires to inhabit with you this land that he gives you and if you cast him out, he will cast you out. Then his presence, which through your virtues should inhabit the earth, will once more, by your sins, be exiled into heaven."

Pedahel, son of Ammihud, asked, "Moses, our master, you have taught, 'God can do all things.' If God can do all things, how can any cast him out of the earth?"

Moses replied, "Because all things are in God's control, except the fear of God."

Paltiel, son of Azzan, asked, "Moses, our master, why must we put God on earth; ought we not to join him in heaven?"

Moses answered him, "No one deserves the kingdom of heaven who has not wished to establish it on earth."

While the Prophet in the school of the wilderness inculcated the Torah into the children of Israel, Zagzagel in the school on high inculcated it into the angels and in the Garden of Eden the Holy One, blessèd be he, inculcated it into the Righteous who are above the angels.

The Righteous going to the Garden of Eden passed before the gate of hell and the wicked going to hell passed before the gate of Eden. Adam, exiled in his penance between the two gates, cried to the Lord, "King of the World—whom my sin cast out from the world—when shall my penance have an end?"

The Holy One, blessèd be he, answered, "In the beginning I made but one person mingling the dust of all the places of earth. From your sin has come all people, separating their dust one from another. In the end joining together all the earth's spaces, all people once again will be but one. Then your penance will be done."

Thus covered by the cloud, watered by the twelve rivers and nourished by manna, the Israelites wandered in the wilderness from Tahath to Terah, from Hashmonah to Moseroth, from Haggidgad to Yotbathah, receiving and reciting the instruction of the wilderness.

Now sometimes in the silence of the night Moses went out of the camp seeking solitude that he might, as in the days of the burning bush, make in his soul a desert.

One night as he was seated in a cave—that same cave where later the prophet Elijah meditated—he pled with God, "What have I known of you, Lord? What have I been able to understand? I have seen your throne of splendor, but is your throne yourself? I have seen your face, but is your face yourself? I have called you mighty, strong, merciful; I have called you Truth, Peace, Love! But to give you a name, is it not to diminish you? And to diminish you, is it not to blaspheme you? Are you not above all these things of humankind: power, justice, mercy, truth, peace and love? The name you yourself taught me, the unutterable name that I alone do utter that means, I AM THAT I AM, is it not also too small for your Majesty that is greater even than Being? You have spoken to me in my language, speak to me in yours. You have opened to me 49 gateways to understanding, open to me the 50th, O Lord, so that beyond your throne and face and name I may know you and understand you and see you as you yourself see."

God answered, "Stay shut in the cave of your solitude and look and I will pass by."

Then with eyes that are not of the body, with eyes that are not of the soul, the Prophet looked but he saw nothing except the shadow of a shadow, as it is written, *No one shall see God and live.*

As he came out of the cave, behold, in their open tombs beneath the full moon, all the dead fallen in the desert! Moses said to them, "Alas, alas! for 40 years I pastured Jethro's sheep in the pastures of Midian. I never lost one, and you, my brothers, my sons, whom I led to pasture in the Land of Promise, along the way I have lost you all. God taught you the Torah; despite his Torah you have learned nothing. He aided you with his miracles; despite his miracles you conquered nothing. Will your sons follow me or shall I lose them also? Will they live for the Torah or will they die through it? Will the Lord still desire to perform miracles for them? Lord, Lord, I have brought up in the Torah a new generation; let it not be like the old one! King of the World, let them live, let them live, these new sons! And may you do for them this miracle that they hear you and follow you without any miracle!"

As he drew near he looked at the open tombs: the tombs had grown, the dead had grown. Their shrouds were not in rags, their flesh was not dust; neither the worms of the earth nor the vultures of heaven had been near their untouched bodies. The iron of their swords shone in their hands; the redness of blood glowed in their faces; the light of day came from their eyes. Moses said to them, "What! my brothers, my sons, over your bones I prophesied corruption, but God has preserved them alive in death. Did you not blaspheme the name of the Lord?"

"We sang his name in the Divided Waters," they answered.

"Did you not give your gold to the Golden Calf?"

"We gave it to the Tabernacle," the dead answered.

"Did you not refuse the Land of Promise?"

"We sought it and you still seek it. Return, Moses. When you have found it, you shall lead us there on the other side of death."

Then the Prophet cried, "Lord, Lord, no human knows you. No human shall know you. But since these, who were born in ignorance and in idolatry, have known you enough to attain you in the grave, they who are born in your light shall know you enough to go wherever you go."

Now in the 40th year after they had left Yobathah for Abronah, and Abronah for Ezion-Geber, the Israelites returned to camp at Kadesh-Barnea. On the eighth day of Ab the crier cried, "Dig yourselves graves."

They dug themselves graves, lay down in them and all night groaned aloud. The next day at dawn the crier cried, "Let the living get up from the dead." But all rose up, the generation of sin was no more.

Then Moses said, "Let the generation of the Torah enter into the Land of the Torah."

CHAPTER XX

THE NEW SONS

The Torah, according to our masters, does not tell us to run after duty; it is enough that we await it. It commands, "If a bird's nest *chance to be before you* in the way, you shall let the mother bird go free." It commands, "*If you meet* your enemy's ox or his ass going astray, you shall bring it back to him." But concerning peace, it commands, "*Seek out* peace."

Thus Moses sent a message to the King of Edom saying, "The time is come when the Lord our God shall deliver to the children of Israel the land promised to their ancestors. Our way crosses your country. Let us pass through in peace. We will not use our weapons, we will not touch your wells, your harvests nor your cattle for rivers follow us to quench our thirst and the manna of heaven satisfies our hunger."

The King of Edom having refused, Moses did not wish to force him, although he had the aid of the Lord. For the sake of peace he chose the longer way that goes by Seir.

As the Israelites were folding up their tents, Miriam the prophetess died. Like the sinners of the wilderness she was not allowed to enter into the Land of Promise because she had slandered the Prophet. He grieved over her death, his head covered with ashes, crouching barefoot on the ground, his mantle torn, with his brother Aaron and his mother—the aged Jochebed who having given birth to 600,000 Israelites through the deliverance of Moses, survived the High Priest, the Prophetess and the Prophet and she alone followed to the end the sons of her 600,000 sons.

Thus, all three wept.

Why, ask our sages, has the Holy One, blessèd be he, put a bitterness into our tears? In order that this bitterness shall hurt our eyes and prevent them from weeping too long, for so great is our grief over death that if our eyes could weep like our hearts, they would lose their sight by the excess of tears.

Now all three were silent, for they had no more tears for their grief. In their silence, there came to them the mingled and increasing voices of a multitude. "What is this tumult?" asked Moses.

"Our master," replied Aaron, "do you not know that these new children of Israel have tender hearts? They come in compassion of our grief."

"If they came in compassion," murmured Jochebed, "they would come in silence."

In truth our elders have said, "Only silence gives value to compassion."

But already faces grimaced and fists threatened in the entrance of the tent. "Miriam's well has dried up. The twelve rivers have ceased to flow; there is no more water for our children! No more water for our beasts! Why are you here weeping the dead, when the living die of thirst? Water! Water! We must have water!"

Never yet had Moses been angered to the point of cursing his people. His patience equalled his love and fled wrath, for wrath takes away wisdom from the wise and sight from the seer. But on that day he forgot his patience.

Every good thought gives birth to an angel, our rabbis have said. This throng whom thirst had made to rebel had thought of the thirst of their animals, but the Prophet could not see the angel born of that thought, for rage blinded him.

"What," he cried, "you come to insult the mourning for her who watered your thirst during 40 years! I have set over you chiefs of tens, of hundreds, of thousands, princes of tribes, elders. If you need water, go ask them for it!"

"No, it is you, our leader, who must give it. Who has led us into this desert without wells? Is it they or you? Give us water!"

"I have none."

"Perform a miracle."

"A miracle! They will not live without miracles! And if I cannot perform one?"

"You divided the sea, according to what you told us, and you can no longer perform miracles? For our parents, who sinned, you could and for us, who have not sinned, you cannot? Give us water, Prophet, or you shall have stones!" And already they began to stone him.

Rising up from his grief, he fled to the Tabernacle. God said to him as before, "Speak to the rock and water will gush forth."

He walked in the desert of Meribah, rage swelling his nostrils. His rod trembled in his hands and his soul cried out, "Forty years have I taught them and see what they know! Because they have been one hour without drinking! As soon as their bellies speak their hearts are silenced. O generation of rebels and blasphemers!"

All howled after him, "Strike this rock, strike that one; why choose? For a miracle all rocks are good enough." But he, in the night of his fury knew not where to strike. Then the multitude stopped. "Think you to lead us to the end of the world? We will wait no longer. Water at once! Water, or you die!"

"Rebels, sons of rebels! If I gave you to drink all the torrents of the mountains, you would still thirst for cursing and sacrilege."

"Strike, strike!"

"But how do I know whether the water will flow?"

"He knows not, he knows not! Why are you not dead with our parents, if you know no more than they? You slew them during 40 years; now it is we whom you would kill."

He struck and a single drop of water dropped from the rock. "Are we sucklings? Would you have us suck? Water! Water! Rivers! Seas!"

Then his mighty fist rose up to heaven and his wrath fell, shattering the rock. A sea of blood gushed, flooding the desert.

All cried, "God is no more with him, he is Prophet no more."

The rock cried, "Why have you struck me?"

God also cried, "I told you to speak to the rock; did I tell you to strike it? I told you to lead my people; did I tell you to insult them? If they are sacrilegious blasphemers, why should you go where you go? You teach doubt to them who have faith; you erase my name in the hearts of those who seek me; and you expect them to find me?" He commanded the rock, "Be healed of your blood; let water cleanse you." The blood covered the sand of the desert with roses and the water reflected them.

Instantly all cried, "Moses is our Master, is Moses the Prophet?"

As he returned, alone, to the Tabernacle he groaned to the Lord, "I have sinned, Lord; anger clouded my heart. I no longer hoped that you would perform a miracle."

"Why should I not? Am I weary of being God?"

"For 40 years I had implanted in them your faith; I hoped that they would believe without miracles."

"You, yourself, did you believe without miracles? You would curse them because they are as you were? Did I not say to you in the bondage of Egypt, 'Show reverence to them, the people'? For so great is the people that I permit the High Priest to turn his back on the holy Ark where I am enthroned to bless the people."

"Yes, Lord, I have sinned. Will you pardon me?"

God was long silent, then he said, "Lead them."

Now the cloud that chased before it the nations, burned up the serpents, filled the valleys and flattened the summits, had left standing in the desert three mountains: Sinai, for the Lord, Hor, for the High Priest and Nebo, for the Prophet. When they arrived at the mountain Hor they camped at the foot of the mount. The Lord said to the Prophet, "Moses, my servant, I have to give you a message that weighs on my heart."

"What is it, Lord?"

"Aaron your brother, like Miriam, has sinned by slandering you before my face. He must die as did the generation of sinners."

"When I, a sinner, have pardoned, will you not pardon, Lord? He has sinned but once and your mercy is great."

God answered, "Was it not through a single sin that death came into the world? How can I spare the High Priest alone when 600,000 corpses are stretched out in the wilderness? Aaron your brother has never had any secret from me. I do not want to have any from him. Announce to him that he is about to die. I cannot tell him myself. I have not courage enough, though I am God."

Then Moses' heart broke into tears. He pleaded, "Lord, Lord, you are King over every creature. The will of every creature is in your hand, but how can I be willing to announce his death to Aaron my brother, who is older than I?"

"Lead him up on the mountain with his son Eleazar. What must be said, you shall say it to him."

Since God himself obeys the Prophet, can the Prophet not obey God? The next day, before the hour of the morning when his custom was to await the people, the princes, the elders and the High Priest, Moses rose and said to Joshua, "Go and announce to the people, to the princes and to the elders that they are to meet me at the dwelling of Aaron my brother."

When he had come there, Aaron asked him, "Why is it you who come today, my brother?"

"I have to bring you a message from God."

"What is it?"

"I will tell you when we have gone out."

Aaron put on the eight vestments of the High Priest and followed him.

Now the custom was when they went up in procession to the Tabernacle that Aaron walked on Moses' right, Eleazar on his left, the Elders and the princes on each side and the multitude behind. That day Moses changed the accustomed order. He placed himself on the right, Eleazar on the left and Aaron between them. Seeing this, the multitude rejoiced, saying, "Moses gives up his place! Aaron is the more holy!" for they loved Aaron more than Moses. His part not being justice, he could listen wholly to the promptings of his heart. He went from hearth to hearth teaching goodness to the children, explaining their duty to the grownups; not satisfied to make peace between people and God, he also made it between the wise and the ignorant and between the ignorant and the wise. In memory of the marriages he had reconciled, 40,000 sons in Israel were called Aaron and when a sinner was about to sin, he would stop short, thinking, "If I sin, shall I be able to look without shame into Aaron's eyes?" So on that morning all were joyful.

When they arrived at the Tabernacle, the High Priest started to go in. "No," Moses said, "we will go outside the camp today."

When they were outside, Aaron asked him, "What is this message from God?"

He answered, "Wait until we are on the mountain." At the foot of the mount he commanded the Elders and the princes and the people, "Remain here, I will go up with Eleazar and Aaron. When we have heard God, we will come down again."

While they were going up, Moses sought in his heart for something that could lead Aaron to the thought of death. Thinking of a person's soul, he said to him, "Aaron my brother, has the Holy One, blessèd be he, entrusted anything to you?"

"Yes, indeed; he has entrusted to me the altar and the Tabernacle on which are the twelve loaves of Israel."

"Perhaps one day he will ask you to give him back his trust! Has he not entrusted you with something else?"

"What? I pray you tell me."

"A light."

"More than one," answered Aaron, "He has put in my charge the seven lights that shine in the sanctuary."

Not daring to speak to him more of the soul, Moses said again, "Truly God has named you well, the simple of heart."

As they conversed together, a grotto opened before them. "How beautiful it is," said the Prophet, "let us go in." He trembled, for now he must tell the High Priest to take off the priestly vestments. "Aaron my brother, perhaps there are graves in this grotto. Would it be right to defile your holy garments by going near?"

"You are right, Moses my brother. Let me take them off and invest with them my son Eleazar." Then the Lord performed a miracle: as Aaron took them off one by one to vest them on his son Eleazar: the triple-crowned tiara which expiates blasphemy, the breastplate with its double clasp that expiates forfeiture, the golden ephod that expiates idolatry, the coat with bells that expiates slander, the straight miter, the sash of secret folds, the shirt without folds and the breeches of fine linen that expiate pride, theft, lying and concupiscence, the Holy One, blessèd be he, to hide the nakedness of his High Priest from earth and heaven, covered him with the eight vestments of Divinity which are Majesty, Might, Glory, Magnificence, Justice, Mercy, Truth and Love.

When Eleazar was dressed in the splendor of the priesthood, Moses commanded him, "Wait here." Then, alone with Aaron, he entered the grotto. They saw there a couch, a table and a lamp which angels were lighting.

Then Aaron said, "Moses my brother, why hide from me longer the message from God? Even if it should be my death, I am prepared for it."

"But, my brother," Moses answered, "was I prepared to announce it to you?"

"Alas, alas! that you did not speak sooner, Moses, when I still had near me my mother, my wife and my other children!..."

The Prophet tried to console him, "Your son Eleazar has walked in your ways. You will live on in him. He shall be High Priest after you and to the end of days all the high priests of Israel shall be, from son to son, sons of Aaron. But what shall my own son be? He has in no way cherished the Torah that I have taught. No prophets shall come forth from my loins. I shall be alone after my death, alone as in my life. And see, angels await you. Your son accompanied you here. They will accompany you from here."

Aaron answered no more. The angels stretched him on the couch in silence and in silence he went where go the angels.

When the Prophet came out of the grotto, Eleazar asked him, "Moses, our master, where is my father?"

"He is with God."

They went down again, but when the multitude at the foot of the mountain saw them return without Aaron, they cried, "What have you done with him? They have killed him! They have killed him! Eleazar wanted his tiara; Moses wanted glory. Murderers, murderers, you have killed him!"

Once again the stones rained from the ground to stone them. Suddenly in the height of the mountain, the grotto opened and the angels came forth soaring through space, their wings bearing Aaron's sacred body. The Lord, intoning praise, chanted, *He that walked in righteousness, I have wanted him to enter into peace.* And the angels made answer, *Goodness was on his mouth, love on his lips. In peace he has gone out, into peace he has entered.* Knowing that God himself had taken back his High Priest, all mourned him.

Skirting the land of Edom, Israel continued its march through the wilderness. As Miriam's well of twelve rivers had disappeared with her, so had the cloud of glory and its twelve splendors with Aaron. Seeing for the first time the stars of heaven, more than one Israelite fell on their knees and worshiped them. All lamented, for the thorns and wild beasts were no longer burned up before them. All were terrified for the peoples, no longer dazzled by the cloud's splendors, asked themselves, "Is this, then, the people whom its God protected? Its God abandoned it; we can destroy it."

Now Amalek lay in wait for them, for he is always there when Israel weakens. He fell upon the Israelites. The Levites repulsed him, but in spite of the victory, the murmuring broke out again, "How long is the way! We had almost arrived and because a king of Edom refused us passage, of necessity we must retrace our steps! Must we, like our ancestors, wander 40 years in the wilderness?"

Moses chided them, "You have angered the Lord against me."

They answered, "For our ancestors you were a Pharaoh crueler than Pharaoh. Why did they follow you? We will no longer follow you!"

Then among the tribes of Gad, Simeon, Asher and Benjamin a cry rose up, "Let us save ourselves from slavery, let us return into Egypt!" Folding their tents, they left the camp and fled in eight days of haste right to Mosserah. The rest pursued them.

"Lord, Lord," groaned Moses, "shall Israelites shed the blood of Israelites?"

But God answered not. Before the trembling face of the Prophet, armed brothers hurled themselves on their brothers. And for seven days and seven nights, his head covered with ashes, crouching with bare feet on the ground, with his cloak torn, Moses the victor mourned over his victory.

Again they went forward. The complaining began again, "Where are the grapes that Caleb brought back? Where are these trees from which flows honey, these fields watered with milk? Manna, always manna! Manna in the morning, manna in the evening, manna on the Sabbath, manna week in and week out! How long shall we have no other food but this accursed manna?"

Then all the serpents that Aaron's cloud had stupefied during 40 years awakened from their torpor in the wilderness. Before the Israelites, behind the Israelites, to the left, to the right, as far as their eyes could see, they saw the slow heaving of the reptiles rolling and unrolling their knotted coils from which came forth in myriads the red spines of their venomous fangs.

Why, asks Rabbi Judan, were they punished by serpents? Because when God said to the serpent, "You shall eat of the dust of the earth," the serpent complained not, but when he said to Israel, "you shall eat of the manna of heaven," Israel complained. What then more fitting than the serpent to chastise Israel?

The reptiles wrapped themselves round their legs, twisted their backs in their glaucous folds, stifled their breasts in their slimy embrace and spat into their mouths the venom of their fangs.

Nevertheless, the Israelites did not perish; thickets of serpents in a forest of serpents, they remained upright, still marching on and swollen with their stings, suffocating in their torture, they groaned, "Lord, Lord, we have sinned; Lord, Lord, we repent."

Then the Lord said to Moses, "How many times did you ask me to forgive their parents before renouncing hope of forgiveness for them! Will you not implore me a single time for these?"

"My heart implores you, Lord," answered the Prophet, "but my mouth no longer dares. When you have forgiven them, will they stop their sinning? Are they not just like their parents? Their parents slandered me; they slander me. Their parents rebelled; they rebel. Their parents clamored for Egypt; they clamor for it. Their parents refused manna; they refuse. There will always be Korahs and Dathans and Abirams among them. Must I begin anew what I had not finished? I am weary of sin, I am weary of forgiveness."

"My son," God answered him, "are you sure that in all things they are like the others? The others slandered you through hatred of you, these through love of your brother. The others rebelled because they saw your faith, these because they saw your doubt. The others all wholly clamored for Egypt; most of these have punished those who clamored for it. They have refused manna? They still sin? People never do enough good to destroy all evil, but they never do enough evil to destroy all good. If the gates of prayer are sometimes shut, the gates of repentance are open always."

To what may this be compared, ask our rabbis? To that king who had a son and a friend. Six times the son sinned against his father and six times the friend obtained forgiveness for him. The seventh time the friend dared not intercede again. What, then, did the king? He gave his forgiveness without being asked for it.

"Make yourself a brazen serpent," God said to the Prophet. "Hoist it on the end of a pole and hold it in the air."

Moses obeyed and it came to pass that each time an Israelite, lifting up his thought toward the Eternal, lifted his eyes toward the brazen serpent, the grasp of the serpents that suffocated him was released and his wounds were healed. When, after passing by Zalmonah, Oboth and Iye-Abarim, they came to the valley of Zered, all the serpents were dead, all the Israelites healed.

And Moses wondered, "Will these be indeed the children of the Torah?"

CHAPTER XXI

THE WAY OF VICTORIES

As he had asked passage from the Edomites, for the sake of peace, so also Moses asked it of Sihon, King of the Amorites and of his brother Og, King of Bashan. "We will not use our weapons," his messengers said to them; "we will not touch your people, nor their flocks, nor their harvests; we will even pay for the water of the wells."

But, cursing the Prophet and the Lord, they answered, "We take tribute from the kings of the Canaanites to guard their frontiers. Because your God, whom we know not, has promised, so you pretend, to give their land to their enemies, should we let them who enrich us be destroyed? I, Sihon, King of the Amorites, send my giants against you. I, Og, King of Bashan, wait for you to come seek out mine, for neither your dwarfs nor your dwarfish God are worth my concern."

When he received these messages, the Prophet trembled greatly, for even to one who puts his trust in the Lord it is permitted to be afraid if he leads men who are arrested by fear. He remembered the return of the spies on the night of Ab when 600,000 Israelites had howled in terror and he thought, "What the fathers did not dare to do beneath the shelter of the cloud, will the sons dare to do when it has left them?" So he assembled the tribes of Israel and said to them, "Sihon, King of the Amorites and Og, King of Bashan, refuse us passage and insult the Lord. I will not hide from you that they are terrible, for their father, the son of Shemshai the rebel angel, was Ahiman the giant whom your fathers dared not attack. Sihon is greater in stature than any tower in the world and is as swift as he is tall. Og is so heavy that, no wooden bed being able to bear him, he has made himself a bed out of the iron of the mountains. Every day he eats 1,000 goats, 1,000 sheep and 1,000 oxen and at each meal he drinks a whole river. By the size of the chiefs, measure their armies. In the eyes of God they are nothing. He delivers them to you, if you dare. But do you desire to march against them?"

They answered, "Lead us on."

Sihon the king, with his army, watched for their passage along the Arnon. The slopes of the valley were hollow with caves where the Amorites hid. The two mountains on either side were so close together that from the summit of one to the summit of the other two people could cry out to one another; but to pass it was necessary to go down and then climb up again over a length of seven miles. When the Israelites came to the crest of one of the two mountains, the other, like a servant that awaits his master, ran to meet them. Just as for their fathers the water had divided, so for the sons the rocks came together. While they walked on the miraculous road without even perceiving the miracle, the Amorite king and his giants, as the Egyptians before were engulfed by the waves of the sea, disappeared into the waves of the earth.

When the Israelites came down to the valley, they were thirsty, but not one complained or clamored to Moses for water. The princes themselves dug the rock with their staffs and as they dug, a river gushed forth bearing in its flood helmets and lances and pikes and shields in thousands. Then they knew God's miracle and with one voice all Israel cried out, "It seems good to you, O Lord, to work wonders. It seems good to us to sing them! Here, here is the well made by the Fathers of the world that the princes of the tribes have sought, that the children of Israel have found." And this song was more beautiful than the song of the Divided Waters.

Why, ask our rabbis, is the name of Moses absent from this, while he is named in the other? Because the Prophet, before, had to chant the song, which the Israelites repeated line by line, for if their hearts were already full of God, their mouths did not know yet how to praise him. Now Moses sang no more; he listened in joy to the instruction in the wilderness multiplied by their voices.

The remnant of the Amorite armies gathered in Heshbon. God thrust a mask of terror on their soldiers and blinded their eyes with this. During the whole month of Elul, while the Israelites were occupying the country, God, in order that the whole world should know that he was with them, stopped the sun in the sky.

In the month of Tishri, after they had celebrated the Feast of Tabernacles, Moses thought in his heart, "They did not fear Sihon, will they not fear Og? Perhaps they will think that God protects him since he has allowed him to live more than 500 years." To test them, he sent spies to Jazer.

They returned saying, "Instead of spying it out, we took the city." Then they advanced into the land of Bashan as far as Edrei, where they came at nightfall. At dawn they cried out, "They have built a mountain in the darkness." This mountain was the giant seated on the ramparts. He held in his hand another mountain. This his hand hurled on the camp of the Israelites, but as he hurled it, it fell back on his head and buried him and his whole city. Thus perished the last of the giants whose guardian angels God had enchained at the same instant as Abraham bound his son Isaac on the rock Moriah. From the banks of the Arnon, as far as the slopes of Hermon, their two kingdoms fell to the Israelites.

Seeing these things, Balak, King of Moab, feared for his country. In truth, he had no need to fear, for the Lord had said to Moses, "You shall not lift up your sword against Moab. From lust are they sprung and in lust they live, but they are descended from

Lot, son of Haran, the brother of Abraham. From them shall come Ruth the proselyte from whom shall be born in the course of the ages my son King David and in the end of days my son the King, the Messiah," for the blood of the nations must be united to the blood of Israel to achieve the union of the world. But Balak did not know whether the Prophet would obey the Lord and knowing that he had once been a shepherd in the land of Midian, he consulted, in order to triumph over him, the Elders of Midian.

They said to him, "His might is not in his arm; it is in his mouth. Take against him one who is strong in his mouth."

Then Balak sent the princes of Moab with those of Midian to Balaam, the son of Beor, in his city of Pethor in the land of the Two Rivers, saying, "Behold, there is a people that left Egypt who have conquered two peoples. They are camped before me; come curse this people so that I may drive them back, for I know that anyone you bless is blessèd and the one you curse is cursèd."

This was that same Balaam, Israel's old enemy, who in Egypt as Pharaoh's counselor advised him to cast into the river all the Hebrew male children so that Moses should die as soon as he had been born. This Balaam was a prophet as great among the nations as Moses in Israel. Moses, it is true, surpassed him in that God spoke to him in every hour of the day and night, while he spoke to Balaam only in the night. But on the other hand Balaam surpassed Moses in that Moses had to say to God, "Show me your ways," while Balaam could say, "I have the understanding of the Most High." For, our rabbis comment, the Lord, not wanting the nations to complain and reproach him saying, "You hold yourself apart from us," gave to them, as to Israel, kings and prophets. Israel had Solomon and the nations Nebuchadnezzar, but Solomon built the Temple and Nebuchadnezzar destroyed it. Israel had Moses and the nations Balaam, but Moses served God and Balaam fought against him. Which is why, after Balaam, God withdrew prophecy from the nations and made it the heritage of Israel.

Having heard Balak's message, Balaam consulted the Lord, who answered him, "You shall not go with them. You shall not curse this people. Who touches them, touches the apple of my eye." But when Balak had sent him nobler messengers and larger presents, Balaam sought God again, who said to him, "Go." And he went, thinking, "How many times has the Lord cursed his people after having blessed them. Today he permits me do what he had forbidden. Now I may curse them whom he has blessed!" The Lord had not changed, for to the one with understanding, he changes never. But, comment our sages, this teaches us that God enlightens us without binding us. When the wicked whom he has enlightened still wish to do evil, he leaves them to their wickedness.

Nevertheless, wishing in his goodness to inform him yet again, the Holy One posted an angel on Balaam's way. Three times Balaam's ass saw the angel and wanted to retrace her steps. Three times Balaam saw him not and struck his ass. Then his ass said to him, "Why do you strike me?" Suddenly he saw the angel, who commanded him, saying, "Go; you shall speak according to the word that the Lord shall put into your mouth." But he did not, or would not, understand what the ass had understood.

Why, ask our doctors, commenting on this, has God withdrawn speech from animals? Because, if the animals could speak, their wisdom would make humankind blush.

Now while Balaam went from the land of the Two Rivers toward Ir-Moab where Balak was to meet him, Moses camped with the Israelites on the plain before the Jordan. He said to them in the joy of his heart, "You have done that which your ancestors did not do; you deserve that which they did not deserve. Thus when we have passed over Jordan, the Land of Promise chosen by the Lord shall be given as an heritage to the people he has chosen. The largest tribes shall receive the largest portions, the smaller shall receive smaller portions. Between families the portion shall be decided by consulting the twelve jewels of the High Priest."

The daughters of Zelophehad, who had been stoned in the wilderness, sought the Prophet saying, "Our father is dead; we have not yet husbands nor have we brothers. Shall we inherit no part of our father's portion and be denied our portion in the Lord?"

The Prophet answered, "God is not like fathers of flesh and blood who prefer their sons to their daughters; he is the father of fatherless daughters; they inherit from him. You thus shall have for yourselves and for your husbands your father's portion and your portion in God."

When they had withdrawn, the children of Reuben and the children of Gad came and said, "Ataroth, Dibon, Jazer, Nimrah, Heshbon, Elealeh, Shebam, Nebo and Beon—the whole of these two kingdoms that God has delivered to the children of Israel—is a good land for cattle. We have cattle. Why should we cross the Jordan? Give these lands to us; we will make of them enclosures for our sheep and in them we will live in abundance."

"What!" cried the Prophet, "you prefer your beasts to your sons? When the daughters whose father violated the holiness of the Sabbath claim his portion in God, you refuse yours and that of your children? In the wilderness you sighed after Egypt. Now, because you tread three acres of sweet grass for the pasture of your flocks, you have found Egypt again and you will go no farther? Is it land or is it God that we have come to seek? Others would fight to destroy the idols and join the world to the Lord—and you would remain here to milk your cattle? Do you not remember the spies that came back with the grapes and casting terror among the tribes, brought down on your fathers the wrath of the Most High? Sinners and sons of sinners, must this people wander for another 40 years in the wilderness for your sins?"

Our sages have said, Let the rich not boast of their riches, for wealth is not in flocks nor in harvests nor in garnered gold. The one who crosses seas and mountains to seek it pursues a void if he seek not God. Thus the children of Gad and of Reuben, because they had bound themselves to their pastures and had exiled themselves from the Promised Land, were the first to be cast off their land when Israel was dispersed into exile.

For they did not listen to Moses. They insisted on possessing the two kingdoms, staying there with their wives, their children and their herds, promising to cross the Jordan when their kin might have need of their help. And the Prophet had to yield, but once more bitterness and anguish were in his soul.

Now Balaam coming to curse had arrived with Balak the King at Kiriath-Huzoth. They went up to the high places of Baal and made seven altars. On each altar they sacrificed a ram and a bull. Balak said to Balaam, "From here you can see the utmost part of their camp. Open your mouth and cast on them your curses."

Meanwhile Moses in the Israelites camp thought in the distress of his heart, "We had almost arrived. Shall we go farther? Two tribes abandon God; will the others follow him? Seeing those two well provided, will they have courage, will they have faith? If they have neither courage nor faith, will the Holy One, blessèd be he, give them strength?"

In the high place of Baal, the prophet of the nations opened his mouth to curse, but his mouth, despite himself, proclaimed, "Balak, King of Moab, called me from Aram, out of the mountains of the east, to curse Israel. But I come from the places from which Abraham departed laden with blessings. How can I curse Israel? And Israel goes to the places that Abraham found laden with blessings. How can I curse Israel? One may enter a vineyard if the guard sleeps; but the Eternal does not sleep and Israel is his vine. How can I curse Israel? Brought forth from Egypt by the hand of his God, he rises up like a leopard and stands as a lion; he shall not lie down till he quench his thirst with victories and be drunk with the blood of the peoples accursed. How should I curse Israel? Blessèd is he that blesses him and cursèd is he that curses him!"

Thus spoke Balaam and Moses and the world heard his voice. Then Balak said, "What have you done? I called you to curse my enemies and, behold, you have blessed them!"

"I could not curse them," Balaam answered.

"Come," said Balak, "let us go to the field of Zophim at the top of Pisgah. From there you will see only the last lines of their camp. Perhaps there you will be able to curse them." They went up and made seven altars on Pisgah. On each they sacrificed a bull and a ram. Balak said to Balaam, "Now cast your curses on them."

In the camp of the Israelites Moses thought in his distress, "And if they do enter the Land of Promise, if they do vanquish the cursed peoples, will they vanquish sin? If they vanquish not sin, will they not be cursed in their turn?"

On the top of Pisgah, Balaam opened his mouth to curse but despite himself, his mouth proclaimed, "God is not a person that he should lie, neither a son of Adam that he should take back his promise. Does he speak and not do his intent? Before he created the world, when he saw the sins of the world, he knew not whether to create, but when in his vision he had seen Abraham, Isaac and Jacob, he said, 'Let there be light,' and put on them the light of his benediction. This light does not go out, for when Israel has sinned, he repents of his sin and for the sake of Abraham, Isaac and Jacob, God pardons his sin. When the world has sinned, Israel repents of its sin and for Israel's sake God pardons it. How should I curse Israel? Blessèd is the one who blesses Israel and cursèd is the one who curses Israel!"

Thus cried Balaam from the top of Pisgah. The world and Moses heard his voice. Then Balak said to him, "What have you done? I called you to curse and, behold, you have blessed again."

"I could not curse," Balaam answered him.

"Come," said Balak, "we will go up to the top of Peor. From there you will see only the shadow of their tents and if you cannot curse them, at least do not bless them." They went up on Peor and made seven altars. On each they sacrificed a bull and a ram. Balak said to Balaam, "Now take back from them your blessing."

In the camp of the Israelites Moses was troubled of heart, "What if God does pardon them and they sin again? If for their sins he throws them out from the land that he would have given them, if he disperses them for their sins over all the earth, will they not disappear from the face of the earth, exiling God from the earth with them?"

On the top of Peor, Balaam opened his mouth to take back from the Israelites his blessing, but his mouth, in spite of himself proclaimed, "How goodly are your tents, O Jacob and your tabernacles, O Israel! They are as valleys that are spread forth, as gardens by the river's side, as the aromatic aloe trees which the Lord has planted and as cedar trees beside the waters. They are dispersed among the peoples and they join the peoples together. From them comes the Messiah who joins them to the Lord. How should I curse Israel? Cursèd is the one who curses Israel, but blessèd is the one who blesses Israel!"

Thus, in spite of himself, he who before had cursed Jacob's children now blessed them. While the Prophet of Israel doubted in his heart, the prophet of the nations exalted Israel in the ears of the nations.

And Moses pled, "Lord, Lord, may the truth be in Balaam's mouth and the error be in my heart!"

CHAPTER XXII

THE IDOL OF MOAB

When Balaam left Balak, he said to the King of Moab, "In vain have I sought to curse them; God blesses them. But their glory, that none in the world can prevent, you can delay. These people are chaste and not lustful. Even in Egypt, in the bondage of Pharaoh, they preserved their modesty. Even in the wilderness, in the idolatry of the Golden Calf, they kept themselves from lewdness. Now the Israelites are camped at Shittim where the springs from Sodom flow that shall not dry up until the day of the Messiah. There are found the daughters of Midian and of Moab whose kiss is pleasing to desire. Let them know these daughters and in the concupiscence of Peor may they forget the Lord."

On Balak's command, tents were set up. Before these, old women were posted who offered the Israelites cloths of linen. "Enter," they said to them, "and you shall find stuffs yet more precious."

They entered and the daughters of Moab and Midian who awaited them gave them garments of purple and blue, poured them wine from which blushed debauch and, if they refused, the water of Sodom in which concupiscence pales. They said, "Why do you hate us? We love you and are beautiful." When the Israelites would have clasped them, the women said, "I will not be yours unless you sacrifice to Peor."

"How could I sacrifice to Peor—an idol?" the Israelite would answer and he would repulse the girl.

Instantly she murmured, with caresses, "Peor is a god who, for all sacrifice, asks that you be naked before him."

At first they sinned secretly beneath the tents of skin, but soon, when their sin went unpunished, they went with the daughters of Moab to dance about the naked idol and the animal cry of their profanity mounted to heaven.

Moses groaned to God, "Lord, Lord, was it then Balaam who was wrong? Was the anguish of my heart truthful? Each new advance is a new trial. Each new trial is a new backsliding. What they never did in the uncleanness of the wilderness they do now that they touch the borders of the land of your holiness. Must I again ask your punishment, I who earlier asked your forgiveness?"

For an answer, as in the days of the Golden Calf, the Lord sent pestilence on them. It went through the camp with green face and body of sores and mowed down the Israelites by thousands. Drunk enough to seize their pleasure even from death, they mingled among the corpses with the daughters of obscenity whom their idol protected.

Now Zimri, son of Salu, prince of Simeon, sought out Cozbi, the daughter of Balak the king, and said to her, "Be mine!"

She answered, "My father has spared me for Moses, in order that through his sin you shall all be lost."

"I will show you that I am greater than Moses." And, taking her by her hair, he dragged her to the feet of the Prophet and cried, "Son of Amram, is this woman permitted to me?"

"You know my reply," said the Prophet.

"Where, then," retorted Zimri, "did you go to find Zipporah, the daughter of Jethro? Did this Midian maiden whom you took to wife in the time of your delights come from the Patriarchs? Why do you forbid us what you permitted yourself?"

Moses paled and was silent. The Elders wept around him and Zimri cried, "Live, if it seem good to you, according to the laws that you have made, but by what right would you enforce them on others? Shall we be your slaves rather than Pharaoh's? Shall we stay, because you have decreed it, apart from the peoples, deprived of all the joys that enrich all the peoples? Shall we destroy all the other gods that command us to take pleasure for service to a sad and solitary God that you have invented in order the better to subject us? Let all know, these gods are my gods and their joys are my joys." And, stripping her veils from Cozbi and stripping from himself his cloak, he threw himself on the naked girl and knew her in full sight of the Prophet and of Israel.

Then Phinehas, son of Eleazar, son of Aaron, the High Priest, cried out, "Moses, Moses, our master, have you, then, forgotten your Torah? Will God's rebuke satisfy his justice if we ourselves do not do his justice?" And beneath the eyes of Israel and the Prophet, thrusting his sharp and shining lance into the bodies of the two clasped sinners, he made of them a single corpse that he raised on high, like a standard, towards the Lord. The pestilence ceased. They ceased from their sins but by then 24,000 Israelites were dead.

"You see, Lord," said Moses, "I am too old. My years are 120. Before, when all the tribes of Israel rose up against you, I rose up against them. Today if one only blaspheme you, I remain mute. I no longer dare punish, nor ask you to punish. I know your Torah no more; I know nothing now but to weep. Permit me to avenge you on Midian, then take from me my burden and let me die."

"Avenge yourself on Midian," answered the Lord, "and you shall be gathered to your fathers."

Why, ask our doctors, did God say, "Avenge yourself," as if it were to avenge Moses? And why did Moses say, "that I may avenge you," as if it were to avenge God? It was because God thought, "Have I need of vengeance?" But Moses thought, "If we had worshiped the stars, would the idol have attacked us? It is the

Lord that he attacks in us." For Israel has sins without number, but it is his virtues for which he is hated.

Why, ask our Elders, did Moses wish to avenge God on Midian? Had not Moab sinned as much as Midian? But from Moab was to be born Ruth the proselyte from whom was to be born in the course of ages King David and in the end of the ages the King, the Messiah. Before Moab could be punished, Ruth must be born.

And why, ask our sages, did the God of mercy permit vengeance on that day? It is because, replies Rabbi Simeon, he who leads into sin is the greatest sinner. Two peoples attacked Israel by the sword, Edom and Egypt; and it is written, *You shall not despise the Edomite; you shall not abhor the Egyptian.* But three peoples attacked Israel by sin: Moab, Ammon and Midian. It is written, *You shall be an enemy to the Midianite. Let no Ammonite or Moabite enter into the community of Israel.* Yet such is the grace of the Lord that Ruth the Moabitess saved Israel and shall save all humankind.

Balaam had prophesied, "Behold this people of God. They rise up as a great lion; they shall not lie down until they drink the blood of the accursèd peoples." This prophecy fell on the nations and their prophet.

Meanwhile Moses, to whom the Lord had said, "Avenge yourself on Midian, then shall you be gathered to your fathers," could have delayed his death by delaying the war. He gave no thought to this, but when the Israelites, those same Israelites always ready to stone the Prophet, knew that they would have to lose him after the victory, they would not go out to battle and lots had to be drawn to constrain, one by one, 36,000 warriors to go out.

Moses resolved not to lead them himself. Doubtless he remembered the proverb, *Do not cast a stone into the well where you have drunk,* for he had found in the land of Midian a wife and cattle. Thus he set Phinehas as captain over the army, putting into his hands the holy Ark where God is enthroned above the two

Cherubim. He also bound on him the breastplate on which the
twelve jewels of the tribes foretell the future and garlanded him
with the golden chaplet on which is written the name of the Most
High. Then he commanded him, "Go, zealous servant of the Lord.
Go, Phinehas my son, you who have recalled his Torah to Moses
your master. That which you have begun, it is yours to finish."

In the month of Tebet they returned bringing back immense
spoils of jewels and arms which none had touched so that they
might be equally divided between all the tribes. Reminding themselves they were fighting for God, every morning they had placed
on their left arm the holy phylactery, but waging against idolatry
a humane war they had encompassed the cities on three sides only
so that the enemy could, if they would, escape.

By the sorcery of Balaam, the five kings of Midian, and Balaam
himself, thought to save themselves by rising up into the air. But
Phinehas shot up toward them the name of the Most High on the
golden frontlet and, like six birds pierced by six arrows, they had
fallen from the sky. Now the prophet of these nations, bleeding,
hanged, stoned and burned was but a stinking cinder from which
came forth serpents. The venom of these serpents was so laden
with malevolence there was enough, unto the end of the world,
for all the sorcery of all the sorcerers.

Finishing the tale of victory, Phinehas said to the Prophet,
"Your warriors have remained pure. When they entered the houses
to take the spoil, they veiled the daughters of Midian in order not
to see them. Nevertheless if it pleases you they will offer to the
Holy One, blessèd be he, a sin offering, for when they approached
the women to veil their faces they felt desire in their flesh."

"What!" cried Moses, "you have not slain the women? Was it
not they who vanquished us? Do you want them to vanquish us
again? Sinners a hundred times defiled by sin, do you think you
are strong enough to live with the Lord in the land that he will

give you without killing the idolater and his idols? Tear up the high places, shatter the altars, burn into smoke their wooden and brass statues. Do you think that to eradicate the abomination it is enough to annihilate things without soul? No, upon all Canaan I hurl my anathema. Let the men and the women, the old and the young, without any escape be put to the edge of the sword. On the land of the Eternal let only God and Israel remain."

Thus cursed the agèd Prophet and rage swelled his nostrils. When at night he had returned into his tent, God said to him, "Why have you hurled the anathema, my son? Am I a God whom the death of a sinner rejoices? Ought I not to love mine enemies as people are to love theirs? Have I not ordained that Israel shall help me perfect the world, not destroy it?"

"But in order that it shall help you," answered the Prophet, "must it not be preserved from evil and the evildoer? When it sins, the nations of the world rejoice, saying, 'God's love for Israel will be blotted out.' "

"No," answered the Lord, "all the nations of the world will not blot out my love for Israel. If I have tried my people more than all other peoples, it is because I try only the strong. If I bless them more than all other peoples, it is because more than any other have they sought me out. For idolaters are idolatrous in their mother's womb, but Israelites believe in me before they are born. Thus it is that one day, in the end of time, all Israel shall be before me as the disciple before the mentor and shall receive the secret of my revelation to give it to humankind and to angels, for in that day the angels shall be less near to me than Israel."

"If it be so, Lord, why hurl your wrath against your children? Why must I wrest from you ceaselessly your forgiveness for them?"

"My son, did I not command you, 'When my face is justice, let yours be mercy'? I wished to measure your mercy before I forgave.

But your mercy has wearied before mine and your justice is severer than my justice."

"Was I not right in using severity, King of the World, so that the instinct of evil should vanish from the world."

"Who, my son, has created the instinct of evil? Have you not said it is I? I have made good and evil, and evil for the sake of good. I have mingled in people, angels and animals. Without angels, what would animals become? Without animals, what would angels become? Moab is a product of lust, but Ruth shall come from Moab, and David from Ruth, and from David the Messiah. Do you not see that without Satan the world would perish?"

As to this, our Elders tell us that Rabbi Johanan cried out one day, "Alas, alas! Satan has burned the Temple and massacred the righteous and dispersed Israel among the peoples. The Holy One, blessèd be he, permits the Evil One still to dance in our midst!"

From one Sabbath to another the rabbi fasted and Satan was delivered up to him. He filled his mouth with lead and shut him up in a cauldron. But all passion ceased in the hearts of humankind. No child was any more conceived and images of the Lord were born no more on earth. Then Rabbi Johanan reopened the cauldron and said, "Let Satan be free to accomplish God's work."

Moses, when he had heard the God of goodness defend the Evil One against him, cried out, "Who can understand your ways, O Lord? You wish that Satan live but that humans serve you?"

"I wish," answered the Lord, "that Satan live so that humans master him and that humans serve me to master Satan. For by giving unto humans the passion to perfect themselves, I have given them more than perfection.

"Now I have said to you, my son, all you can comprehend. You have vanquished the idol of Moab. You have avenged yourself on Midian. Make ready your soul. Your day is about to close."

CHAPTER XXIII

THE TWILIGHT OF THE PROPHET

Moses went outside the camp and, looking on Jordan in the distance, said to the Eternal, "Lord, why is my death so near?"

"Did you not ask to die?"

"Let me first cross over Jordan; then I will go to be gathered to my ancestors."

The Eternal answered, "You shall not cross the Jordan. The others shall enter the Land of Promise, but you shall not enter in."

"Why, Lord? I have led them this far and they are to go in without me? Think what I have suffered for them: My distress in Egypt. My hardship in the wilderness. Your love that I inculcated in them in pain, may I not teach it to them in joy? Have I not celebrated your Sabbath? Fasted 40 days and 40 nights to receive your Word? For your name opposed those with sin? Shall I have no reward? Will you belie your Torah where you have written, *You shall give the laborer his hire before evening*? Will you be like the king of flesh and blood who dismisses servants when they grow old? Weak as I am, can I not still lead them? Where will they go without me? Without me what will they do? Will you keep them, Lord, when your prophet is no longer there to keep them?"

"I found one prophet;" answered God, "I will find others."

"If I cannot lead them as Prophet into the Land of Promise, let me enter it as the disciple of another."

"You shall not enter it."

"Let me enter it like whomsoever among them."

"You shall not enter it."

"If I do not enter alive, let me enter dead; let my bones rest there."

"You shall not enter it. I have said that the whole generation of sin shall die without entering in. All are dead. Miriam is dead, Aaron is dead. Like them, without entering in, you shall die."

"Have I not walked in your ways, Lord, all the days of my life? Have I not fled iniquity and deceit and forsaken all delight to be yours alone? What sin have I committed to deserve your wrath?"

"Seek your sin."

"By the burning bush when you wished to send me to save Israel, I said to you, 'Send another.' "

"That sin was the child of a greater sin."

"By the rock of Meribah I refused in my anger your miracle for your people."

"That sin was the child of a greater."

"By the idol of Moab I commanded that all the Canaanites, with the women and the children, the young and the old, should be put to the edge of the sword."

"That sin was the child of a greater sin."

"Lord, Lord, what is this greater sin?"

Then God said, "You doubted me, I forgave you. You doubted yourself, I forgave you. But you have doubted Israel, you have doubted humankind; thus you shall not enter this Land of my Promise. Israel is encumbered with blemishes, but from where do you come if not from Israel? My prophet is my people; my people are my prophet. They are cowardly, perverse, envious, lustful, lying, thieving, murderous and blaspheming, but what are you if not human? What you have understood of me, should not others one day understand also? If with all your heart, soul and might you hoped they would comprehend, would you have said, 'Send another'? Would you have refused my miracle, hurled forth your anger, commanded extermination?"

"I believe in them. I do believe in them, Lord, but so often they disappointed me. My heart wavers and what I hoped, I no longer dare expect."

"Had you, then, not seen in me eternity? The righteous help God by their justice, by their love, but above all by their patience. Israel also will be disappointed a thousand times, yet they will wait to the end of days. Because Israel waits until the end of time, humankind shall wait with Israel, God will wait with humankind."

"Am I God that I should have the patience of God?" cried Moses. "Where is the person who has never sinned before your face? Will you not pardon me my sin, King of the World, for the sake of the many times I implored your forgiveness when my people sinned? Shall I not obtain for myself your mercy which I obtained for them?"

"Ten times I have judged you, ten times condemned."

"Has my prayer not changed your judgments?"

"Then your prayer was for all, but today you plead for yourself only."

"Lord, Lord, let me enter into the Land of Promise."

"You shall not enter it."

"Let me enter, Lord; say that I may enter it!"

"Importune me no more. Your doom is sealed. Your death is ordained."

"If I must die, King of the World, at least permit me before I die to know whom you will put in my place so I may instruct the one whom you have chosen as to what he must do for you after me."

"Return to the camp. You shall be told whom I have chosen and shall instruct him. When you have instructed him you shall be gathered to your ancestors."

When the Prophet was in the Tabernacle, he said to the Eternal, "God of my Fathers, you Who search the spirits of all mortals, Who knows who is humble and who is proud, who is gentle and who is wrathful, give your children a leader worthier than I to succeed me. Let this one have all strength, all wisdom, all goodness, all justice, all love in order to lead them where I have not been able and to arrive where I have not been able to come."

"My son," the Holy One, blessèd be he, answered, "this perfect person that you ask of me shall not come for them till the end of days. But to each day its own task is sufficient and to each task its own design. I have perceived your grief. I would have preferred that your sons after you should be my servants, but they have not enough cherished my Torah, which is yours; they will not inherit your spirit, which is mine. Whoever tends the fig tree shall eat its fruit! Joshua, your disciple, has venerated and followed you, has cared for you and served you from dusk to dawn and from dawn to dusk. Let him have his reward. While you still live, let him teach the Torah in your place so that later it cannot be said, 'He who knew nothing while Moses lived now pretends to know all.' When the disciple has become the teacher, you shall be gathered to your fathers."

When he had been told God's message, Joshua wept and tore his garments and threw himself at the feet of the Prophet. "Alas, alas!" he cried. "You wish, then, to leave your people? Who shall lead it? Who shall pray for it? Where shall I find food and drink for it? Where shall I find for it justice and love? What will the nations of the earth say? That he is no more whose mouth was invincible, the possessor of the divine name, the Prophet of the Lord. That he is there no more to defend the children of Israel against their enemies and against their God, to invoke the merit of the Patriarchs when they sin and to bring down from heaven the forgiveness and the wonders that made them all-powerful. Son of Amram, what will become of your people if now all the peoples rise up and cry, 'Let Israel be blotted from the face of the earth!'?"

"Joshua, my son," Moses answered, "do not demean yourself. You know what I myself was when God chose me. Do you think he chose me for my strength or my virtues? His grace has given me everything. I was nothing without him. I, too, said to him, weeping, 'Send another.' Yet I went. You shall go, even as I."

Then, in memory of the 36 years Joshua had sanctified by abasing himself before him, Moses, raising up to his own high place his disciple, sanctified from the first day of Shebat to the sixth day of Adar, 36 days.

To honor him the first week, Moses stopped his explanation of the Torah when Joshua entered and did not continue his discourse until he had sat down. Then when all had gone, Moses taught him the last laws, "Explain to the children of Israel that they are to give to the Levites cities in which to live in their own parcel, for the portion of Levi is the portion of God. Let them choose also cities of refuge where the unwilling murderer shall find asylum, for the blood shall not be shed of one who shed blood unwillingly."

Often Joshua was filled with fear, "What shall I do," he asked, "when the Jordan is passed and the lands are to be portioned out? They who receive a mountain will clamor for a valley. They who receive a valley will clamor for a mountain!"

"Fear not," Moses answered, "the people I entrust to you is still in its childhood, but it is the people of God. Love it like a child and say to it, 'Love God.' If sometimes it defy you, think on the sweetness of loving the children of the Lord."

During the second week, Moses laid his hands on Joshua's head and looked long into his face. It came to pass that the spirit of God that was in Moses came to dwell in the spirit of Joshua and the splendor of God that shone on the face of Moses shone on the face of Joshua, but Moses kept in his spirit and on his face the spirit and the splendor of God.

The Prophet wished to set his disciple at his side in the School of the Torah but Joshua at first refused, saying, "Is not the disciple's place at the feet of his teacher?" Moses wished that Joshua should explain the Torah before all but at first Joshua refused, saying, "Is not the silence of the disciple the praise of the master?"

The Prophet answered, "None here is greater than you." When they were seated side by side on the golden throne, Moses proclaimed an ordinance and Joshua commented on it, then Joshua pronounced an ordinance and Moses commented on it. Their thought was the same and their word was the same, and Joshua's countenance shined like the sun.

During the third week, Moses left his tent preceded by his disciple. A herald cried out before Joshua, "Come all to hear the new prophet, who rises up over you!" Seeing the disciple before the master and the herald before the disciple, all Israel wept saying, "We will not go! Woe to the land whose king is a child!"

But Moses answered, "God's love is upon children." He urged the Elders, princes and the chiefs of thousands and of hundreds and of tens and the whole people to honor Joshua. And he urged the disciple to sit alone in the court on the golden throne while he himself sat on a bench at his left.

Joshua wept, saying, "Why has this greatness come on me?"

During the fourth week, Moses rose up every night in the middle of the night and went in to the tent where Joshua still slept and prepared for him his shirt of fine linen and shook the dust from his miter and coat and sandals that he placed near his bed and went to draw water for his cleansing and to arrange the benches in a semicircle in the court of the swaying walls.

While the Elders, princes, Levites and the people learned to go up to the new master, the old master served him and dressed him. Joshua, ashamed and trembling, flung himself at Moses' feet, "O my master, will you not shorten my days by leading me into sin?"

Moses, raising him up, answered, "Why do you think it sin to accept from me what I accepted from you? Have I not taught you, 'Honor your disciple as yourself'? Should I not do that which I have taught?"

During the fifth week Moses served Joshua but Joshua wept no more. Moses wanted to set him on his throne, but Joshua had already seated himself there. One day when Moses entered while Joshua was speaking, Joshua did not interrupt himself, nor rise. The whole congregation cried, "Why, Joshua, do you remain seated while your teacher stands?" In their indignation the disciples would have killed him.

Joshua rose up, saying, "Moses, my master, I did not see you. Will you forgive me?" He made him sit on the bench at this left.

Everyone cried, "Let Moses, our master, teach us."

He answered, "I cannot."

And as they all cried; "Teach us, teach us!" a voice sounded from the sky, "Listen to Joshua."

During the 35 days of Joshua's exalting, Moses, hoping God would allow himself to be swayed, asked everyone to intercede for him. First he went to Joshua himself, saying, "My son, remember my patience in teaching you, night and day, my wisdom and the wisdom of God. Pray to the Lord for me, so that with you I may enter into the Land of Promise."

At these words Joshua in his grief struck his hands together, but as he began to pray, Samael, the archangel of death, closed his mouth, crying, "How dare you rebel against God's command?" And Joshua held his peace.

Then Moses had sought out the High Priest Eleazar, the son of Aaron and said to him, "My son, remember my courage in defending your father Aaron against Korah, Abiram, Dathan and the princes of the tribes and the princes of the Levites when they wished to oust him from his priesthood. Pray the Lord for me, so that with you I may enter into the Land of Promise."

But when Eleazar began to pray, Samael, the archangel of death, closed his mouth, crying, "Do you presume to command God?" And the High Priest held his peace.

Then Moses sought out the aid of Caleb, Phinehas, the Elders, the princes, and the chiefs of hosts of thousands, of hundreds and of tens. Samael closed their mouths, every one.

In the last week he implored all Israel one by one, saying, "Remember the anger of God against your parents and my supplication that warded off from them his wrath. How many times was Israel about to perish and my prayer saved them? Go, now into the Tabernacle; in your turn pray for me so will God take pity on me and let me enter the Land of his Promise with you."

Lo! When the multitude uttered their pleas to God from the sanctuary, 148 hosts of angels led by Samael came down from heaven and seizing their prayers in flight prevented them from rising up to the Lord.

During 35 days, Moses, each day humiliated yet more deeply before his successor, sought to delay his death. On the 36th day when he heard Joshua declare these words, *Praise to the Holy One, blessèd be he who makes his delight the righteous in their instruction!* the Prophet saw in the cloud of glory the presence of God whisper into the ear of him who had been his disciple and dictate to him his words. And Moses understood them not.

When Joshua had finished, he said to him who had been his master, "Son of Amram, repeat the lesson to the children of Israel."

But the Prophet, having not understood, could not repeat it. Then he asked, "Joshua, our master, what then has the Lord revealed to you?"

And Joshua answered him, "When he spoke to you face to face, did you tell me what he told you?"

And then, understanding that his day was done, the Prophet groaned to God, "Lord, Lord, I would rather die than understand no longer and only envy them that hear the word of God." And he prepared his soul for death.

CHAPTER XXIV

THE KISS OF GOD

It was the sixth day of the month of Adar. In the middle of the day a voice sounded from the sky, "Moses, Moses! There remains to you only one day more to live in this world."

"Why is my death so near?" groaned the Prophet.

"Have you not twice asked to die?"

"Lord, Lord, you showed me your might on Sinai and your strength in the ten plagues of Egypt; you showed me your mercy the day of the Golden Calf and your love by the manna in the wilderness. Let me still live to tell your glory!"

That night the Prophet said 1,500 prayers and recopied the Torah 13 times on scrolls of parchment, thinking, " 'The Torah is your life and the prolonging thereof.' Perhaps it will prolong mine."

But on the morning of the seventh day of Adar the voice sounded in the sky, "Moses, Moses! there remain to you but six more hours to live."

Moses answered, "First let me bless Israel; then I will go to be gathered to my ancestors." Then he assembled the multitude and pronounced blessing over them.

He spoke over Reuben: "Let him be rewarded for saving Joseph and not punished for defiling Bilhah. Let there come forth from him heroes of might and of the Torah."

He spoke over Judah: "Let him be rewarded for speaking for Benjamin and not punished for polluting Tamar. From him let there come forth kings of war and kings of peace."

He spoke over Levi: "He massacred the Shechemites, but he did not worship the Golden Calf. He was overeager to avenge Dinah, but at Shittim his eagerness avenged the Lord. Let priests without blemish come forth from him, and from him the forgiveness of the Eternal."

He called down on Joseph abundance of dews, on Zebulun abundance of purple and gold; to Dan, Gad and Issachar he promised increase of flocks, to Naphtali fish, to Asher olives and to all, the joy of the worship of the Lord. But to Simeon he promised nothing, for Simeon had sinned with the daughters of Moab.

Our rabbis tell us that although Moses was not the first to bless on earth, his blessing was the most fruitful, for Noah blessed Shem his son, but cursed Ham; Isaac blessed his two sons, Esau and Jacob, but his blessing divided them; Jacob blessed his twelve sons, but in his blessing he chided Reuben; while Moses, since he was unable to bless Simeon, did not name him—in order not to curse him. Thus his blessing was perfect.

When Moses ended, a voice from heaven sounded, "Moses, Moses! There remains to you but four hours to live in this world."

The Prophet pleaded, "Lord, Lord, let me bid farewell to Israel; then I will go to be gathered to my ancestors."

Then he read to the tribes the whole Torah and gave a copy to each of the tribes saying, "Keep you the Torah and may it keep you. Let no word, no sign be changed until the end of the ages, so you may live unto the end of the ages."

All cried, "We will keep it until the end of the ages so may it keep us!"

The thirteenth Torah that Moses had copied was taken by the angel Gabriel to bear it back to heaven.

Then the Prophet said, "Often I chided you because of the Torah, forgive me."

They answered, "Often we angered you for your Torah, forgive us." And they forgave him and he forgave them.

Then he said again, "When you have entered into the land of Israel, remember my bones that shall think of you, and say, 'Alas, alas! the son of Amram who ran before us like a steed has fallen, he has fallen in the wilderness!' "

They all groaned, "Moses, Moses our master, what shall we do without you?"

He answered, "God remains with you. It was not for me, but for you that through me he wrought his wonders. Do not put your trust in those of flesh and blood. You perceive that they are nothing, for death takes them. The Lord will send you other prophets. Listen to them, follow them, but if ever one of them claims to be God, believe him not, for God alone is God."

They all cried, "Hear, O Israel, the Lord is our God, the Lord is One."

Then the Prophet turned to Joshua and asked, "Do you wish further light on the Torah? For I go; you shall not see me more."

"Moses, our master," answered Joshua, "have I ever left you for a single moment since I have been your disciple? Have you not, night and day, explained to me the Torah? I asked you everything, you did tell me all."

"Since you have no more requests to make to me, let me make one to you. Embrace me." And Moses embraced Joshua twice and twice he blessed him, saying, "Let peace be on you and on Israel!"

As he blessed him the voice sounded from the sky, "Moses, Moses! there remains to you but two hours to live in this world. Go up alone into Nebo and die in light."

Why, ask our rabbis, did God wish that Moses die alone? Because Moses' grave was to remain unknown; for if anyone had known the place, they would have worshiped his tomb as an idol and Moses as a god. And why, ask our rabbis, did God wish that

Moses should die in light? Because if he had died in darkness, they would have said, "God was able to take him from us because it was night. In the full light of day we would have taken him back."

The Prophet still delayed, held in the arms of his mother, his sons and his wife.

Again the voice sounded, "Moses, Moses! Go up into the mountain; there remains to you but one more hour to live!"

Then he tore his cloak, covered his head with dust and said, "Happy the people of Israel that is not ever to die! Farewell, my brethren, my sons; we shall meet again in another world."

And as all rent their garments and fell groaning with their faces in the dust, he went up alone into the mountain, wailing aloud.

None, say our sages, die before their day. But however late they die, they die too soon for their desire. The Prophet, having twice asked for death and knowing from the mouth of God that he had but one more hour to live, would not yet accept death.

Abandoned by humans, he now pleaded with the mountain and the wilderness, heaven and earth. Climbing up Nebo he said to them in the midst of his sobs, "Plead for me the pity of the Lord; may he save me from death."

But the mountain answered, "May he first have pity on me. Has he not written, *The mountains shall depart and the hills be removed?*"

Heaven and Earth replied, "May he first have pity on us. Has he not written, *The earth wears out like a garment; the heavens dissolve like smoke?*"

The wilderness answered, *Everything returns to its own place; all was dust, to dust shall all return.*

The Prophet groaned, "Where can I go? With whom can I plead? Once a Pharaoh was my slave; I delivered a whole people of slaves; I ordained the Sabbath and the Fast; I decreed life and death; the Torah took my name; I commanded the whole world;

I changed the order of things. To the heaven that rains down water I said, 'Send bread,' and manna fell. To the earth that makes the bread to come up I said, 'Let water come up,' and water came. God himself obeyed me. I said to him, 'Rise up,' and he rose; 'Stop,' and he stopped. I said to him, 'Punish,' and he punished; 'Forgive,' and he forgave. What am I now? An old man that begs and to whom none listens any more."

"It is the law of all flesh my son," God answered him. "You have had your day; now let others have theirs. Whose son are you? Amram's. Whose son was Amram? Kohath's. And Kohath was the son of Levi and all were the sons of Adam and all died like Adam. Why should you not die?"

"Lord, Lord," Moses implored him, "since you can do all things, can you not also spare me death?"

"If you did not die in this world, my son, how would you live again in the other? I have made ready for you all the joys of Paradise. On earth you commanded the 60 hosts of Israel; in heaven you shall command the 55 hosts of the Righteous who shall walk in the ways of my Torah. Moses, your days will pass, but your life shall not pass. You shall have no need of roof or cloak, or bread for your hunger, or oil for your head, or sandals for your feet, or sun or moon for your seeing for I will shelter you with my splendor. I will clothe you in my splendor. I will feed you on my delights. I will bear you upon the wings of my glory. On your face shall shine a light whose shadow only has shone on your face on earth."

But Moses did not yet submit. Again he groaned, "King of the World, King of the World, if you do not permit me to cross over Jordan nor see the Promised Land, permit me to live, Lord, so that I can see the world! If you will not permit me to remain a human, let me live like a beast of the field, let me live like a fowl of the air, but let me live, let me live. O let me not die!"

Thus did the Prophet implore and the mountains and the sea trembled. The firmament and the abyss cried out in terror. All the voices of the universe howled in anguish, "Is God, then, about to destroy the universe?" For the prayer of Moses was like a sword to cut down and tear the worlds, containing in its lament the ineffable name that created the worlds. Then the Lord ordered all the angels to shut the gates of all prayers so that the prayer of the Prophet should not be received and the angels sang, "Glory to the Holy One, blessèd be he; Who knows no favor nor injustice and makes death equal for all mortals."

Moses had now come to the top of the mountain. God said to him, "Why do you tremble, my son?"

"I am afraid."

"Of what?"

"I am afraid of Samael; I am afraid of death."

"Look before you."

Moses looked and God said to him, "See this land beyond this river? It is the land that I promised to Abraham, Isaac and Jacob when I swore, 'I will give it to your children and to your children's children.' You shall not enter into it, but you may see it."

As the Prophet looked, the Lord put into his eyes such powers that he saw the whole land from the Jordan to the sea, from Hermon to the wilderness and every place in the land from the portion of Naphtali to that of Simeon, from that of Reuben to that of Dan, from the vines of Carmel to the stones of Sodom, from the roses of Sharon to the pastures of Gilead. As he looked, the Lord put into his eyes such force that he saw not only every place, but every age in every place: Jericho falling at the blast of the trumpet; Samson bearing the gates of Gaza to the hills of Hebron; Deborah on Mount Tabor raining down stars on the armies of Sisera; Samuel at Ramoth anointing with oil the head of Saul; David gathering in the brook Elah flintstones to slay a giant; Solomon leading the Ark of Sinai into the Temple of Moriah in the midst of the singing of songs.

The Prophet murmured in the joy of his heart, "Lord, Lord, you keep your promise and your children keep theirs. You have led them into the land of your choice and they have led you there to dwell."

But after the victories he saw the defeats; after the sins, the punishments: Ahab and Jezabel prostituting themselves to the idols in the high places of Samaria; Manasseh commanding a prophet's body to be sawn through on the trunk of a terebinth tree; Ahaz laying down his bed, defiling the Holy of Holies beneath the wings of the Cherubim; Jehoiakim in the Valley of Topheth feeding the flesh of his son into the flaming belly of Baal. On them came the helmeted horsemen of Nebuchadnezzar with their hairy lancers and their sinewy archers; and Titus with his Romans, his Syrians, his Arabians, his Getæ, bearing sling and spear and pike and catapult, extinguishing in blood the seven stars of the candlestick and dragging into exile the groaning remnant of the twelve tribes.

Moses, in the anguish of his heart, groaned, "Alas, my children! What are you doing? Where are you going? You are driven on the roads like cattle with rings of brass through your nostrils! You are dragged in chains and behind you the children of Edom lift up their heads in blithe rejoicing! You are tracked down barefoot with bleeding hands through the valleys and through the mountains, beneath the sun and beneath the storm, without a home, without a land, without rest! O Judah, O Gad, O Benjamin, O Ephraim, you hunger and have no more manna, you thirst and have no wells! You wander and have no more a pillar of cloud to lead you by day nor a pillar of fire by night! Lord, Lord, can you suffer the shame in which you have put them? Why deliver them from bondage, opening for them twelve pathways through the sea, changing sand into gardens and rock into fountains and light up your mountain and from it proclaim your Law to your people, only to blot out yourself by blotting them from the world?"

Lo, beneath the eyes of the Prophet, filling all space, appeared a gigantic Temple! Its courts were of onyx and beryl, its gateways of jasper and sardonyx, its beams of emerald, its roofs of topaz, its columns of agate, chrysolite and amethyst, its altar of ruby, garnet and sapphire. And before the Temple waited the Messiah.

Moses whispered, "Is that the Temple of heaven or is it the Temple of earth?"

"Moses, my father," the Messiah answered him, "this Temple that you see is neither of earth nor of heaven. It is the Temple of heaven that the earth shall build." As he spoke, all the seas opened and all the pathways of the seas, all the peoples redeemed from sin went up toward the Temple waving palms and singing songs. After all the peoples came, all the dead of all the ages and all lands returned from the Garden of Eden or from Gehenna waving palms and singing psalms. Before the peoples walked Israel, singing psalms and waving palms.

The Messiah said to the Prophet, "Moses, my father, how could you have entered into the Land of Promise? It is not only beyond Jordan, the country that you sought, it is beyond love, beyond hope. See, it is the whole Earth of all people." As he spoke in the vast Temple, a vast table rose up over all the mountains and plains, over all the continents and seas. Around the table all the peoples were seated for the last Passover. Adam poured them out wine pressed from the grapes of all vineyards and portioned to them bread harvested from the corn of all fields. All celebrated the last Passover and sang with Adam and with Israel and with the Messiah, "Hosanna! Hosanna! The days have come full circle. God is One! All peoples are One! Peace to all people in heaven, peace on earth to God.

When, like the mists of a dream engulfed by night, the visions of the future were devoured by the midday sun, the Lord said to Moses, "I have ordained death for all mortals. For Israel alone have I ordained life in order that humankind shall live and that there shall live the Messiah. If you desire it, I can change my decree: you shall not die, but Israel shall perish. Your day shall be stayed, you shall be eternal, but the Messiah shall not be born."

Moses answered the Lord, "You are a God of mercy, King of the World. Let the Messiah come and let the people live; let Israel live and let me perish."

When the Holy One, blessèd be he, saw that the Prophet accepted death, he said to Gabriel, "Go, gather up his soul."

But the archangel answered, "He has led your people with your power in his hand and your word in his mouth. He has dried up the sea, shattered the Golden Calf. I will not give death to this Righteous One."

Then God said to Michael, "Go, gather up his soul."

But the archangel answered, "He alone utters your ineffable name. You have made him more than an angel and almost a god. I will not give death to this Righteous One."

Now for 120 years Samael had waited for Moses to be delivered up to him. He said to the Eternal, "I will go take his soul."

The Eternal answered him, "Would you even dare to approach him? What part of his sacred body could your myriad eyes even look on? His countenance? It has seen my countenance. His hand? It has received the Torah from my hand. His feet? They have tread the threshold of my Splendor."

"Nevertheless, I will go," Samael answered. He grasped his sword, belted himself with cruelty, clothed himself in anger and came before Moses.

When he saw him, the Prophet, standing on the summit of the mountain, traced in the air with his radiant fingers the four signs

of the unutterable name and like motionless lightning in translucent space, the name remained suspended. Samael was hurled to
earth and sought to flee like a wounded serpent. But Moses' knee
was on his throat and the angel of death was about to die when a
voice cried from the heaven, "Moses, my son, slay not death. The
world has need of him." Samael fled and the Eternal appeared.

He said to the Prophet, "Do you think, my son, that I would
have suffered to see you die like other mortals? Lay you down.
Cross your feet one above the other. Cross one hand above the
other." Moses obeyed. "Shut your eyes." He obeyed.

Then God, calling to himself the Prophet's soul, murmured, "O
my daughter, I ordained that you should dwell for 120 years in the
body of this human. Leave it now; the hour is come."

But the soul replied, "King of the World, I know that you are
God of all spirits and hold in your hands the souls of the quick
and the dead. You have created me and you have put me in the
body of this Righteous One. Is there in the world a body as pure
as his? I love it; I do not want to leave it."

"My daughter," God answered, "do not hesitate to obey me. I
will place you in the highest heaven beneath the throne of my
glory with my Cherubim and my Seraphim."

"King of the World," said the soul, "Your angels themselves
have become corrupted. When Azza and Azael came down from
the heights to couple with the daughters of men, you had to chain
them between earth and heaven for their punishment. But Moses,
from the moment you allowed him to look on you face to face,
has no more known flesh. Thus I desire to remain with him."

"Do you, then, fear Samael?" the Prophet asked his soul.

"In no way. God will not deliver me to Samael."

"Do you dread having to weep my death as Israel will weep it?"

"In no way. The Lord has delivered mine eyes from tears."

"Do you fear being sent into the gulf of hell?"

"In no way. God has promised me the joys of heaven."

"Then go, my soul, where the Lord summons you and bless with me his love."

The Eternal gathered up the soul from Moses' mouth and the Prophet died in the kiss of God.

As soon as he was dead, a cry resounded in the camp of the children of Israel, wailing, "Woe, woe; he is dead!" On the next day the manna did not fall. Israel, that had wept for Moses 30 days before losing him, lamented over him 90 days.

The earth also wept, wailing, "The Righteous has left human-kind."

Heaven also wept, wailing, "Heaven has left earth."

The Eternal cried, "Moses, my son, you have said to me, 'There is no other God in heaven or earth.' I say of you, 'There shall be no other Moses in Israel.' " And God wept.

Now while all wept for the son of Amram, his mother Joche-bed would not believe in his death. She went to ask Sinai, "Sinai, Sinai, have you seen my son?"

"I have not seen him since he made the Torah come down on me."

She went to ask the wilderness, "Wilderness, wilderness, have you seen my son?"

"I have not seen him since he made the manna come down on me."

The sea answered her, "I have not seen him since he changed my waves into dry land."

The Nile answered her, "I have not seen him since he turned my waters into blood."

Jochebed journeyed through all the world crying out, "Where is my son? Where is my son?"

The Prophet went up towards the Eternal. When Adam saw him, he said, "Why do you go higher than I? Was I not created in the image of God?"

But a voice sounded, "He is greater than you. You lost the glory you received of God; what he received, he preserved."

Noah said to him, "Why do you go higher than I? Did I not escape from the Flood?"

The voice sounded, "He is greater than you; you saved yourself alone; he has saved his people."

Abraham said to him, "Why do you go higher than I? Did I not feed them that passed by?"

The voice sounded, "You fed them in the inhabited places; he fed them in the wilderness."

Isaac said to him, "Why do you go higher than I? Did I not see Moriah the Splendor of God on the rock?"

The voice sounded, "You saw it and your eyes failed; he saw it and his eyes see it still."

Jacob said to him, "Why do you go higher than I? Did I not wrestle with the angel and vanquish the angel?"

And the voice sounded, "He is greater than you; you vanquished the angel on earth; he vanquished the angels in heaven."

Then Moses went up and seated himself beneath the throne of glory. And seated beneath the throne of glory, the Prophet, with God, awaits the hour of the Messiah.

Additional copies of this book may be obtained
from your local bookstore
or by sending $15.45 for a paperback copy, postpaid,
or $22.45 for a library hardcover copy, postpaid,
to:

Hope Publishing House
P.O. Box 60008
Pasadena, CA 91116

CA residents kindly add 8¼% tax
FAX orders to (818) 792-2121
VISA/MC orders to (800) 326-2671